Never Alone

Never Alone

*A Story of Survival
Under the Gang of Four*

by

Dr. Sung Ming and Min Tsu
with A. F. Harper, editor

Beacon Hill Press of Kansas City
Kansas City, Missouri

Copyright 1983
by Beacon Hill Press of Kansas City
Printed in the United States of America

ISBN: 0-8341-0848-8

Cover art: Royce Ratcliff

Unless otherwise stated, all scripture quotations are from the *New American Standard Bible*. Permission to quote from the following copyrighted versions of the Bible is acknowledged with appreciation!

The *New American Standard Bible* (NASB), © The Lockman Foundation, 1960, 1962, 1968, 1971, 1972, 1973, 1975, 1977.

The *Holy Bible, New International Version* (NIV), © copyright 1978 by the New York International Bible Society.

The *Bible: A New Translation* (Moffatt), copyright 1954 by James A. R. Moffatt. By permission of Harper and Row, Publishers, Inc.

10 9 8 7 6 5 4 3 2 1

Contents

Foreword		7
Introduction		9
1	The Cultural Revolution Hits Home	11
2	What Happened in My Family	23
3	In the Prison	34
4	Deepening Persecution	47
5	Ignored and Attacked Again	59
6	Life in a Prison Hospital	70
7	Released but Not Free	79
8	Min Tsu—My Wife's Story	89
9	Serving in Our Homeland	110
10	Seeking a New Life	119
11	America	128
12	He Has Taught Us	134

Foreword

This is the true story of a Christian family from mainland China. They were caught up in the persecution during the years of the Cultural Revolution.

All of the facts have been reported just as they occurred.

THE EDITOR

Introduction

Ever since we met . . . the author, his wife, and I . . . in their homeland, I've had troublesome thoughts that will not go away and disturbing questions that will not be stilled. Such as . . .

What makes them so different anyway?

Is it that they have reached beyond themselves for those resources it takes to be real Christians anywhere?

Have those same divine resources not only enabled them to survive a literal hell on earth but also made them incredibly strong?

Can you decide to do that without being forced to? to actually get into a commitment you can't handle without God's help? when something divine simply has to happen?

Is my commitment requiring much divine to happen or can I pretty well handle myself?

Do only those Christians who undergo severe persecution achieve their level of faith . . . that quality and depth of commitment . . . or is it open to anyone else? If so, what are the terms?

Must I be deprived of that privilege simply because I happen to live in a society that has let me be a Christian so far without too much pressure . . . and with nothing you could call sacrifice?

I sure wish I had been praying more for them. I will from now on. That's a promise.

I just wonder if I would risk my life for my Bible, not to mention my songbook.

I want to learn more about gratitude.

I want to learn more about faith and obedience and courage. But do I really?

And finally, "Must I be carried to the skies on flowery beds of ease, while others fought to win the prize and sailed through bloody seas?"

So as you move through these pages you will be confronted with a new and serious spiritual challenge. And you will clearly hear God's promise again:

> *... Strength for the day,*
> *Rest for the labor,*
> *Light for the way,*
> *Grace for the trials*
> *Help from above,*
> *Unfailing sympathy*
> *Undying love.*
>
> PAUL SKILES

Chapter 1

The Cultural Revolution Hits Home

Bang! Bang! Bang! "Open the door. Open the door."
It was nine o'clock in the evening of August 24, 1966. The pounding was loud and rough. Stones, bricks, and mud were thrown against our house. The windows were broken one by one.

It was one of the sudden attacks organized by the "Red Guards." They numbered about 15 million throughout China, mainly high school and college students but supported and backed up by the Central Committee of the so-called nonproletarian class. It was the prelude to what the world came to know as the "Cultural Revolution."

We leaped out of bed quaking with fear, wondering what was happening. We could see the street below was filled with angry high school students wearing red arm bands printed with yellow Chinese characters, RED GUARDS.

"Open the door," they shouted. "Quick, you rotten troublemakers."

The door was smashed even while we were hurrying to open it. They poured into our home like the waters of a flood, screaming, "Down with bourgeois class. Down with all exploiter elements. You slaves of Western culture and science, get out of this house. It is time to put an end to all of you. Hands up. Surrender!"

We asked, "What is this? What law have we broken?"

"Shut up," they answered. "You have no right to speak. You have no right to ask questions. Give us all your treasures and keys. Surrender all your official papers and letters. Do you know who we are? We are Red Guards guided directly by our great leader. We are here to search your house."

We quickly picked up a copy of the *Constitution of the People's Republic of China* to argue with them. We said, "We are a peaceful family living here together with our parents. We work as doctors and college teachers. Since we have broken no law, you cannot search our house."

One of the Guards grabbed the copy of the constitution and threw it back into our faces, saying, "How stupid can you be? If you dare resist us, you are breaking the law. We have authority to put you into prison. Will you challenge us?"

Then about 50 Guards scattered into all the rooms of the house. They forced our family into one room, with four armed persons sitting at the door to guard us. We were forbidden to talk. All we could do was to ask God to save us from injury and to close their eyes to what they should not discover while searching the house.

We could plainly hear the sounds of the search. Doors opened . . . trunks and cases overturned and smashed . . . drawers pulled out and emptied. They were digging into the floors, hammering on walls, and drilling into them. The intruders even climbed to the roof to turn up the tiles. The Guards shouted in glee when they discovered something; they scolded loudly if a drawer yielded nothing that they wanted.

Their ransacking included not only the inside of the house but also outside in the yard. They destroyed flowers and plants, digging one hole after another thinking we might have buried treasures to conceal them. Our house and yard looked like a battlefield.

The surprise search included all our treasures—jewels, gold, silver, and money. Our greater concern was that the Guards were looking for documents, letters, certificates, samples of handwriting, and even small handwritten notes—hoping to find proofs to support their false charges against us. They hoped to take away our belongings on the pretense that we were guilty of a crime against the state. If they could find and destroy titles to the property and certificates of ownership, we would be without legal defense when they confiscated our property and took us to trial.

My father had brought great profits to the government through his scientific skills. All of his children had worked hard. All had been especially careful to obey the regulations of the government, knowing that we were suspect because we were not born in a proletarian family. Suddenly we were treated like criminals. We had committed no crimes and had broken no law. Unfortunately, the law had been cancelled in one night. Huddled together in that room, we worried deeply about what they might find and what they would do to us.

That night we thought we knew how Jesus' disciples must have felt when "there arose a fierce gale of wind, and the waves were breaking over the boat so much that the boat was already filling up" (Mark 4:37).

At that mad time almost anything that reflected prosperity or Western culture made one suspect: leather shoes of good quality or modern style; ladies' skirts, dresses, and stockings; men's suits and neckties; pictures or photos found in nonproletarian families; classic Eastern or Western literature, music, novels, records, and tapes; all Western magazines and newspapers, even Western scientific books—all made one an enemy of the Cultural Revolution.

Our home was searched and ransacked by the Red Guards every day for two weeks. Nothing remained concealed and nothing of value was left. The Guards burned all of our books, certificates, documents, drawings, curios, photos, Bibles, and hymnbooks. Even though they could not be used to incriminate us, they also destroyed ancient Chinese relics and Western mementos.

These Red Guards in their teens destroyed everything that they supposed to be useless. But they were too young to know much about what was valuable. They were badly taught and rushed rampant into homes of suspected enemies of the Cultural Revolution. This searching and destroying was called "Totally Destructive Home Searching."

The Red Guards sat in the windows or on balconies singing and laughing while they threw our shoes, clothing, furniture, books, and albums into the fire. They shouted loudly, "Long live our leader Mao and our vice leader Lin. Long live the Cultural Revolution. Long live the Red Guards."

At the end of these two weeks our material possessions of a lifetime were gone. My retired parents were each given only 12 yen (about $10.00) per month to live on. It was a rude shock after being accustomed to the comforts of a professional life and a middle-class income. There was physical stress and mental tension, with no hope for improvement in the future. Life was difficult, but we felt fortunate at the close of each day that we were all together; none of us were in prison.

Our parents worried about their children, and the children worried about their parents' safety. We knew many people who were put into prison immediately simply because the Guards found one sentence in an old letter from a friend that they considered against the present government. Others suffered the same fate when a legal title to property owned under the former government was discovered in their files. This supposedly proved that they wished the return of the former government. Some small excuse could always be found to justify their sudden attack and to prove their charges.

It seemed that everything was gone; but we had Jesus living inside us. Every night we knelt together in the presence of God asking for His protection. Wonderfully He delivered us from dangers one by one. Through our earnest prayers, God shut our persecutors' eyes to some personal papers that were entirely legal but which would have been used against us. At the same time, God comforted our hearts even while we were in great sorrow. The more we tasted bitter persecution, the more we felt sweetness from above.

What God Taught Me

Out of these experiences God opened my eyes and my heart to understand what He was doing for His own. He made us see clearly that all the worldly treasures and successes for which men had labored many generations could be taken away within hours.

Many upper-class Chinese people who did not believe in Jesus could not take these heavy losses. They fell ill after their possessions were taken away; many committed suicide.

Our losses taught me the truths that James knew: "Come now, you rich, weep and howl for your miseries which are coming upon you. Your riches have rotted and your garments have become moth-eaten. Your gold and silver have rusted; and their rust will be a witness against you and will consume your flesh like fire. It is in the last days that you have stored up your treasures!" (Jas. 5:1-3). I began to understand how wise our parents had been when they stored most of their properties in heaven. They had taken care of God's children in troubles and had given happily for the support of the church.

I realized that if we worked only for our own living, it was unworthy and meaningless. I perceived that God's Word will not be changed—not even one dash or one dot. I admonished myself that I should esteem my spiritual life more than my medical career—though medicine seemed to me a very valuable work.

I began to repent of my sins. I examined myself to recollect all the wrongs that I had committed, and I asked for God's forgiveness. The more I repented, the more light I saw. I praised God and thanked Him for His goodness and His justice. He taught me the truths of the Bible: "And He, when He comes, will convict the world concerning sin, and righteousness, and judgment" (John 16:8). Also, "It is time for judgment to begin with the household of God" (1 Pet. 4:17). My spirit said, Amen. We were His. We belonged to His household. God used all of this to help us know His love and His justice, for "we know that God causes all things to work together for good to those who love God, to those who are called according to His purpose" (Rom. 8:28). This was the understanding that came from above. The truth made us happy even in sorrow. We trusted Him and we obeyed Him.

One of Satan's master strokes is to keep Christian people silent. He thus robs the world of the Good News and hinders people from finding Christ. The "Gang of Four" knew this and they tried to shut off all Christian influences. During the 1960s the churches in China were closed. Bibles and hymnbooks were burned everywhere they were found. Preachers and responsible lay brothers and sisters were arrested or forced to do heavy labor. There could be no public worship; no preaching or praying; no reading of Scripture or Christian teaching; no singing or winning new believers. Nevertheless, silent and private prayers were offered to God by His true children.

I knew how the Psalmist felt, and I always sighed deeply when I remembered his words:

> *By the rivers of Babylon,*
> *There we sat down and wept,*
> *When we remembered Zion.*
> *Upon the willows in the midst of it*
> *We hung our harps.*
> *............................*
> *If I forget you, O Jerusalem,*
> *May my right hand forget her skill.*
> *May my tongue cleave to the roof of my mouth,*
> *If I do not remember you,*
> *If I do not exalt Jerusalem*
> *Above my chief joy.*
> (Ps. 137:1-2, 5-6)

In these days we needed the strength that comes from God's Word, but the only access we had was what we could recall. I regretted greatly that I had not memorized more precious verses when I had a Bible to read. I am afraid when we have God's blessings we do not esteem them as highly as we should.

The Red Guards always ridiculed us boldly, "Where is your God now? If God knows you, why does He not come to save you? If you still believe, you had better go quickly to see your God today because you have been spat out by the Chinese people."

We answered no word to the Guards because we believed that God would someday deliver all of us from their evil. Since we were not the first to suffer persecution for our faith, we found strength in remembering other suffering people of God. The Psalmist shouted, "Many are saying of my soul, 'There is no deliverance for him in God' ... [but] ... I will not be afraid of ten thousands of people who have set themselves against me round about. Arise, O Lord; save me, O my God" (Ps. 3:2, 6-7).

Atrocities Witnessed

The Cultural Revolution was a massive political movement—the proletarian class struggling against all nonproletarian elements. It developed quickly and with extreme savagery. During these years there was no education, no normal work, no peace, no respect, no morality, no honor. Instead of good deeds and virtues there was only shouting, screaming, fighting, beatings, robberies, rapes, assaults, suicides, and murders. China was not a nation of human beings but a land possessed and controlled by the devil. The youthful Guards established a "Red Guards' Headquarters" in our house. Up to 20 of them occupied our favorite rooms in which our family for years had shared pleasant times. They forced six of us to live in one small bedroom. It was bare except for two small wooden stools and two little chests for the few old clothes they let us keep. We slept on the floor.

One evening these crazed Guards caught two young people suspected of opposing their orders. They took the accused young men up to the third story of our house to a room that our parents had dedicated as a special place for prayer. The Guards were policemen, judges, and jury at that time. In this sacred place they beat their prisoners with fists, belts, and rods. They cut them with knives. Downstairs we heard the two men crying and shrieking through the night.

The Red Guards laughed loudly, saying, "No beating, no confessing. We are owners of the country. We will beat you to death." Then came the chilling sounds of more blows on bare flesh—thud ... thud ... thud.

At dawn the Guards ordered all of us to go upstairs to watch the penalty they gave to the two young men. We saw them kneeling naked and trembling on the floor. On their backs were bloody gashes from the knives and blue welts from the beatings. On the table was a bowl of salt and water that the Guards rubbed into these bleeding wounds. The victims screamed with pain.

The Guards threatened us with similar punishment if we said one word against them. We longed to leave our house, but without their permission we could not. We were like sheep living among wolves.

During these days a young couple teaching German in one of the universities was forced to explain why they were not satisfied with the Cultural Revolution. They were then insulted and beaten repeatedly. Life became unbearable. One night, alone in their room, they used the lamp and two pieces of wood to form the shadow of a cross on the wall. This was their last Christian witness. In desperation they hung themselves, one on each side of the cross.

Because of the overwhelming pressure of persecution, a young unmarried pianist living with her mother and younger brother, turned on the gas stove and took their lives.

Confucius taught the Chinese people, "There are three things of which the superior man stands in awe. He stands in awe of the ordinances of Heaven. He stands in awe of great men. He stands in awe of the words of sages." The Red Guards wanted to turn the people against this ancient wisdom of their culture. In the fury of the times, teachers in schools, professors in universities, and respected elders everywhere were ordered to crawl on the ground with ropes around their necks. With these ropes the Guards dragged them from one place to another. Passersby were invited to kick them or beat them.

A famous professor of pediatrics was charged with being a spy for America. When he could no longer endure the suffering of being beaten with clubs and scorched with fire, he jumped from a high building and died.

An aged couple were beaten to death by Red Guards, not for personal charges but because they suspected the couple's grown son, a world-famous pianist, of opposing the government.

In the political persecution, the Red Guards were a law to themselves; the police had no control over them. Theoretically the police could protect citizens if the Red Guards committed criminal acts, such as murder, rape, and robbery. But many times even these crimes went unreported and unpunished.

One winter night in 1967 three young Red Guards with cold weather masks on their faces boarded a public bus. They brought with them a young woman with her hands tied, a strong cotton handkerchief stuffed in her mouth, and a cold weather mask over her face. The girl could not make any sound, but tears were in her eyes. The conductor of the bus asked where they were going. Professing to be her brothers, the young men said they were taking her to a psychiatric hospital for treatment of a mental disease. Because the young men were armed with knives, other passengers dared not ask more.

No one questioned them although the girl bounced up and down groaning. Fortunately, the bus driver sensed that something was wrong, so he drove the bus to a police station nearby. Stopping quickly, he shouted to the passengers, "Grab the Guards; rescue the girl."

With the testimony of the passengers and the threat of the police, the three Red Guards confessed that they intended to kill the girl after they had taken her to a suburb and raped her.

A factory in Shi Zhun province produced king-water, a mixture of nitric acid (3 parts) and hydrochloric acid (1 part) used as a strong solvent. The factory employed thousands of workers. Early in the Cultural Revolution, they split into two parties with different political views. At first the two groups only argued and quarrelled. In time they started fighting. First there were fist fights, then battles with self-made weapons—spikes, knives, and daggers. One afternoon guns and machine guns were smuggled in. Many died in the ensuing battle. Hundreds were caught and pushed into the sinks of king-water. Their bodies disintegrated without even a trace of bones remaining. Thousands died, tricked into mortal combat and cheated of life by nothing more important than a theory.

Desecration of tombs all over China was another of the disasters in 1967. Skulls and other bones were exposed on the ground. Dogs, cats, birds, and ants gathered around them. Thoughtless boys pulled these skeletons apart, kicking the skulls like footballs and playing among the bones around the tombs. Some took skulls and bones from the tombs as souvenirs for the home. China looked more like a nation of evil ghosts than a country of human beings.

An acquaintance told us that he had seen policemen shoot their prisoners and then eat the human brains with wine just after the men had died. I was sickened by these reports, but they were told with integrity.

Tien An Mun Square in Peking commemorates Chinese heroes and reflects the achievements of the Chinese people. It is a huge square, beautiful and revered by all of China. On April 4, 1976, thousands of people gathered there in memory of their former premier, Chou En-lai. Jealous leaders of the Cultural Revolution secretly organized a massacre of these innocent people. Suddenly soldiers and policemen with knives and machine guns surrounded the square. No one could escape. They were not even allowed to surrender by holding their hands above their heads.

Human blood flowed like a flooded stream, and corpses were piled in high hills. Many of those who died had come to the square out of mere curiosity.

The ruling leaders charged every dead man with a political crime: he was a "Reactionary Element." The families of these murdered victims had to keep silent. To speak out meant that one was branded as "a relative of the Reactionary Element." To be so charged put their lives in jeopardy.

These experiences happened to one family, or in one factory, or in one square. But similar damage took place all over China in the time of Lin Piao, the vice-chairman from 1966 to 1972, and the days of the Gang of Four. The atrocities continued after the death of Lin Piao until 1976. Thus the Chinese people lived with these agonies for 10 or 12 years. Those who were scarred by the tragedies deserve our prayers.

Chapter 2

What Happened in My Family

Our own situation was becoming darker, and life grew harder and harder. Nearly a year had passed since we had first been attacked. Everyone in the family had become political targets, therefore the Guards could do to any of us whatever they wished. My parents were forced to join other nonproletarian persons to sweep the streets and clean toilets and sewers under the supervision of the Red Guards.

One morning in November 1967 all of the family had gone to work except my mother and a maid who worked in the home. Nearly 30 Red Guards attacked our house again. With unreasoning fury they beat my mother and the maid about their faces and heads.

As a result of her beating, my mother was admitted to the hospital for emergency surgery on her left eye. She stayed in the hospital for three weeks. Before her dismissal we worried about her returning home. If she were beaten again before she recovered, she might lose the sight in her injured eye. There was no place to appeal for justice. There was no law, no protection. No justice, no righteousness. No goodness, no kindness.

In desperation, we asked God to help us. We had written to a Christian young lady, Min Tsu, whom we had formerly known in our city. Six months earlier she had moved to another city to live with relatives there. In reply to our letter she had agreed to help. We then went to the police station to ask a favor. We asked permission for Mother and me to leave the home and go to a relative in another city. Miraculously, the police gave permission for us to go when Mother was discharged from the hospital. We felt glad for Mother's sake but sad to leave other members of the family in the mouth of the tiger.

None of us knew what would happen to us by tomorrow. Anxieties filled our minds. How could we live in another city without income? Could my aging father live through so many beatings? These were heavy burdens, but we thanked our Lord that Mother could depart safely for another place where the Red Guards would not know us.

Because of our political status, it was impossible to take a plane, so we took the train. Unfortunately the jolting of the train so soon after mother's surgery injured her eye again, and she had to be admitted to the hospital for further surgery immediately.

I repined at our fate and murmured about these further misfortunes.

"What can I do?" I cried to God.

I knew my own weakness and felt I could not suffer any more. Some Christians from this new city came to visit us while Mother was in the hospital. They comforted and encouraged us. One good sister sent a precious verse: "Give me your heart, my son, and let your eyes delight in my ways" (Prov. 23:26). I stayed with Mother day and night in the hospital, relieved occasionally by others who came to visit us. Min Tsu came to the hospital nearly every day to visit my mother and to help care for her. Her kind care and happy spirit were as refreshing as a drink of cool water. She did it freely. I could clearly see her love in her goodness. Gradually I realized she was meant to be someone very special to me and to my family.

I had read in the Bible, "And let it come to pass, that the damsel to whom I shall say, Let down thy pitcher, I pray thee, that I may drink; and she shall say, Drink, and I will give thy camels drink also: let the same be she that thou hast appointed for thy servant Isaac; and thereby shall I know that thou hast shewed kindness unto my master" (Gen. 24:14, KJV). This was the criterion of Abraham's servant looking for a wife for Isaac. This verse also became my criterion in looking for someone from God.

I wanted this loving helper for my wife, and she returned my love. When I asked her to marry me, she accepted, though we were both in the same oppressive situation. She asked me nothing except that I bring a Christian faith to our marriage. By that time we had both learned that material wealth could vanish in a moment. But we also knew that the works of God would last forever.

Her faith taught me that "house and wealth are an inheritance from fathers, but a prudent wife is from the Lord" (Prov. 19:14). Also God taught me that "charm is deceitful and beauty is vain, but a woman who fears the Lord, she shall be praised" (Prov. 31:30). Thanks to God for His good gift to me. We prayed together and then went to the official office to register for our marriage, planned for June 1, 1968.

Here let me testify from my experience. If you are wishing and searching for your beloved one, ask God to select the best one for you. Do not choose as worldly people do, asking for property, position, rank, or beauty. Pursuing these earthly values has destroyed many couples' lives and broken many families. We Christians should select someone from inside—the very inside. We need to ask: Is there a firm spiritual base on which both are willing to build? That Christian base comes from the New Testament: "Whosoever heareth these sayings of mine, and doeth them, I will liken him to a wise man, which built his house upon a rock" (Matt. 7:24, KJV).

Through the grace and mercy of God, I testify that we have had success in our marriage. We have been tested by many conditions including prison life. We write these words wishing only to glorify God and to testify that God's Word is trustworthy.

The Vision

God's Word tells us, "And it will come about after this that I will pour out My Spirit on all mankind; and your sons and daughters will prophesy, your old men will dream dreams, your young men will see visions" (Joel 2:28).

What are these dreams and visions? Before I had this experience I could understand very little. When I heard Christians talking about visions, I hoped that someday God would give one to me. But I also heard unbelievers talking about visions as one kind of illusion or a deceiving perception. Some would even say that a vision is the superstition of religion, including Christianity. At that time I could not refute an opponent, because I had not experienced such a communication from God.

Under special circumstances, or when some emergent thing is happening in history, God will show His order or His teaching by visions and dreams. These are very different from ordinary dreams. Maybe the word should be capitalized as a proper noun. Such a Dream is no mere fiction of the mind unrelated to reality. I am a doctor of medicine, and I work in the scientific field. My mind was very clear when I had these experiences. God gave them to me both in times of distress and in my happier days as well.

In the universe there is a magnetic field and an electronic field created by God. In these fields we discover truths that our physical eyes cannot see and our ears cannot hear. This is common scientific knowledge. From my experiences I believe there is also a spiritual field existing in the universe. As we give ourselves to a patient investigation of this area we learn more about the Spirit of

God, the spirit of ourselves, and the spirit of evil in the world. I hope more medical doctors and other scientists will research this field patiently and objectively. We believe that God is a revealing Spirit. If we humbly ask Him to direct us, He shows His power and His secrets. If you are an unbeliever, I encourage you to humble yourself. Ask God to save you from ignorance of His truth. As a medical colleague and a student of science, I encourage you to explore the realm of the spirit.

The Red Guards always sang a song, which has been prohibited in China since 1980.

> *It's red in the East,*
> *The sun is rising.*
> *So rises Mao Tse-tung*
> *Who seeks advantages*
> *For the people.*
> *He is a great savior*
> *Of the people.*

Tung means "the East." *Tse* means "to enrich." *Tse-tung* means "to enrich the East." Mao is his family name. The Guards sang these words to praise Mao as a sun rising red in the East and warming China. They praised him as a great savior of the people. Everyone, young and old, was expected to sing this song of praise to the leader. Everyone was to praise him and bow toward his picture before each meal. In a godless nation it was a form of emperor worship. But God reserves worship for himself alone. The Bible says of Jesus, "He is the STONE WHICH WAS REJECTED by you, THE BUILDERS, but WHICH BECAME THE VERY CORNER stone. And there is salvation in no one else; for there is no other name under heaven that has been given among men, by which we must be saved" (Acts 4:11-12). God's Word tells us that it is a sin to expect too much from any mere human being. There is no Savior in the world other than Jesus Christ.

Only He can save His people from their sins. Only faith in Him and in His teachings can build a good society.

On August 5, 1968, my fiancée, Min Tsu, and I went out for some relaxation. It was a very hot day, and I was tired. As we came back that afternoon on bus No. 25 I closed my eyes to have a short rest. Suddenly I saw a vision. It was as big as a wide movie screen. On it were red Chinese characters, against a light blue background. The color was as red as blood:

Frantic	Tung's
Typhoon	Sides
	Falling Down

I knew clearly that "typhoon" meant a political hurricane, wild and terrible. I also understood that the "savior" who was making great mistakes now would go down and all who sided with him would also go down. This was my first experience to see a vision.

I told Min Tsu about it, and we prayed that we might always be on God's side and in God's will. We knew that the message of the vision was in accord with God's Word: "I have seen a violent, wicked man spreading himself like a luxuriant tree in its native soil. Then he passed away, and lo, he was no more; I sought for him, but he could not be found. ... But the salvation of the righteous is from the Lord; He is their strength in time of trouble. And the Lord helps them, and delivers them; He delivers them from the wicked, and saves them, because they take refuge in Him" (Ps. 37:35-36, 39-40). At the time I did not know that the frantic typhoon would be blowing on us to the spilling of blood.

Twelve years later as I write these lines, the public press in the United States verifies the vision that God gave to me. I read these headlines:

"We Really Are Villains, Half of the Gang of Four Admits"

"A pragmatist, China's new party chief has been a sharp critic of Mao"

"Mao's Widow Receives a 'Suspended Death Sentence'"

"Hua resigns as Chinese party leader"

I am grateful that God showed me the future of my nation and the fate of those authorities when their power was at its peak. When I read the news about the Gang of Four, I could only kneel humbly in the presence of God and say: "How unworthy and low I am. You revealed this vision to me and made me understand that You are the only One who controls the heaven and the earth."

Arrest

On August 31, 1968, we got an official paper from the government for our marriage. We went to a restaurant with my mother and brother for a dinner of celebration. It was a very simple meal, and we were quiet but very happy.

On September 5, we went to the home of a relative for a visit. On the way, we had an interview at the government employment office and I was assigned to work as a doctor in a small hospital in that city. We then went to the housing agent and were assigned a permanent room for living.

When we arrived at my relative's home about 5 p.m., he had no cheerful greeting for us. With a strained look on his face, he just said, "Come in. Sit down."

Before we could be seated, about 20 people from my hometown, accompanied by several local Red Guards, rushed in and surrounded me. They shouted, "Hands up. You are under arrest."

They bound me with rough ropes and cuffed my hands behind my back. They then took me out to the patio and ordered me to kneel down on the concrete. I demanded of them, "Why have you caught me as you would a criminal? I have not committed any crime. We have the official certificates from the police office to move here."

In reply they shouted, "You and your mother have planned to escape the supervision of the Red Guards. This is the most important law that you have broken. Tonight we shall put you in the prison because your arrest has been approved. Sign your name on this paper—the paper of your detention."

They continued, "There are many other crimes that we have found. You should confess. You must write down all that you have done."

It came like a bolt of lightning. I had no choice but to sign my name to the paper. My wife and I were then brought in a police car to a jail in the city to which we had just moved. There we were separated. I did not see her again for nearly three years.

As I entered the door, a guard ordered me to bend over, and he took everything I had in my pockets. After a little while he took off my handcuffs and ropes and led me to a room. It was early autumn and the weather was very warm. Twenty people were squeezed into that small room about 8 by 12 feet. It was now eight o'clock but I was not hungry. There was only a terrible thirst. I asked for a drink, but not one drop of water would be given. How could I bear it! I had never dreamed of being imprisoned, but here I was—without sympathy and with no valid reason for being there.

As I stepped through the heavy wooden door into that room dimly lit by a single five-watt bulb on the ceiling, I was stunned by the scene before me. The bare floor was covered with the sleeping, sweating forms of other prisoners. Along the wall, to my right, I saw a sink at nearly floor level that was used to collect human waste. It was carried out every morning and dumped by two prisoners.

As the newest prisoner, my assigned place on the floor was beside the sink. I could not sleep. I thought of my wife whom I had just married and of my mother still suffering after her eye surgery. I thought of my own prospects. I could not pray; the turn of events was too sudden and too unbearable. Tears came from my eyes and the sweat oozed from my skin making the floor wet. I could see nothing outside, except for two or three stars through a high window and a shaft of light through a peephole in the jail door.

Odorous the stink, hot the room, depressed the mind —and so many mosquitoes! It was the life of a prisoner that I was to experience for 33 months.

The next morning I was taken out for questioning. At that time, the police were also the lawyers because there was no law—only military rule. I was questioned three times during that week.

On the same day that I was taken into custody, my mother waited until 11 p.m. for Min Tsu and me to come home. She was worrying about us when suddenly she heard a heavy knocking. She opened the door and a crowd of nearly 30 Guards rushed in to search our room. They struck Mother mercilessly on both ears. Then having finished their search, they left her alone in the room.

After 1 a.m. of the night I was arrested, the police released my wife. She rushed from the police station and caught a night bus home. When she reached our house about 3 a.m. she saw no light, so quietly opened the door. Switching on the light, she saw my mother slumped in a chair. The shocking events were too much to bear. Mercifully her sorrow was cushioned by a state of semiconsciousness. She struggled to regain consciousness. When she recognized my wife, Mother began to cry. Quickly Min Tsu put her arms around her while she reported what had happened. They wept together with no one to comfort them. My wife knew that Mother needed food, so she forced back her own tears and prepared food that they ate before they rested.

After I was put under arrest, Red Guards came every day to question Min Tsu and Mother. My wife asked them for the money (500 yen) I had carried in my pocket, but they refused to surrender it. At first they said, "There was no money in his pocket."

But my wife knew their plan was to keep the money for themselves, so she questioned them strongly. At last they said, "The money in the pocket of the Reactionary Element cannot be returned to you even though you are his wife. We assure you that he will be sentenced to at least 15 years in the prison. We will not press charges against you because you are so young. You were deceived by him and his family. You should reject him and all his relatives. We can cancel your marriage because you have had the official marriage paper for only five days. You can save yourself if you follow our instructions and tell us all that his family has done."

To these words my wife said nothing in reply. She knew they were trying to trick her.

The evening of the sixth day of our detention in the city, the police came to tell my wife that the next day I would be sent back to our native town and that my mother would be sent back within one week. Again the Guards pressed her to forsake and betray me.

I was handcuffed and taken to the railway station early the next morning. In the rail depot they ordered me to sit on the concrete floor, publicly exhibited to other passengers and workers in the station for ridicule. My wife came hoping to see me once again and to try to give me some clean clothes. But no way. She was told, "A young man with handcuffs has already gone."

She went back home with a heavy heart. But as she made the trip a song came to her mind:

> *Be not dismayed whate'er betide;*
> *God will take care of you.*
> *Beneath His wings of love abide;*
> *God will take care of you.*

Again and again the words sang themselves in her spirit and she was comforted. When she got home she told Mother, "I did not find him, but I have peace in my heart."

Right away my wife prepared the luggage for Mother's departure. One week later Mother began the trip alone by train to our family home. From that time there was no further communication with my family. Min Tsu began two years of life as a fugitive until she was captured and put into prison. During these years everyone in our family suffered bitterly, but thanks to our faithful God, His grace was sufficient for us. We lived with the 23rd psalm:

> He restoreth my soul: he leadeth me in the paths of righteousness for his name's sake. Yea, though I walk through the valley of the shadow of death, I will fear no evil: for thou art with me; thy rod and thy staff they comfort me *(vv. 3-4, KJV).*

Chapter 3

In the Prison

After the journey by train to our native city, I was ordered to sit handcuffed on the sidewalk outside of the railway station. About midnight on September 16, 1968, a police jeep took me to prison where I would be held for the next 33 months.

In my prison the walls were concrete, the floor was wood, the door was iron bars. There were three small windows near the ceiling, and no artificial light inside. There were no beds, no chairs, no tables. We were forced to sit and sleep on the floor.

The prison was built in a U shape, divided into 16 rooms of different sizes. I was put in Room No. 11, about 12 by 24 feet, with 50 other prisoners—persons guilty of murder, rape, assault, and robbery. It was dangerous to be confined with them, and I accepted a smaller food portion just to avoid their anger and mistreatment. Each of us had just enough space to lie on the floor. We were called by numbers instead of by our names. Our only possessions were the clothes we wore, a towel, and in the winter a blanket that was shared with another prisoner.

We were not allowed to talk with each other, and no books could be taken inside except *Mao's Works*. The guards argued that we could be truly reformed by studying the works of Mao. They tried to make us accept the idea that the words of great Mao could be "redemptive" to all who believe them. We were forced to read and memorize these writings. If we could not recite them, we were punished by prisoners. To tell you the truth, I found that his words could not comfort my inner mind. I eagerly needed the Words of Life with real power, not the words of knowledge.

Those who memorized Mao's words did so just to show their captors that they were learning Mao's teaching. They wanted the guards to believe that their minds and thinking were being influenced by it. The truth is, the more they learned, the more skilled they became at convincing the guards of their conversion. They spoke whatever was expected of them, but in their inner minds they were unchanged.

By this strategy, they could be set free more quickly, but after several months they would be arrested and brought back because they had committed another offense against the criminal law. A young prisoner, about 18 years old, told me one day privately that he had been in this jail seven times. He said, "To learn Mao's words made me understand how to write and how to answer, so that I could be released seven times."

Such behavior made me clearly comprehend that only Jesus can reform one's real inner mind to make him a good man. I know that God can save a man if he believes in Jesus Christ. But I have not seen strict laws, observance of the words of man, or punishment that would cause men to abandon their evil ways.

Saved from Anxiety

In prison, one day often seemed like a whole week to me. There was nothing of interest to challenge the mind. Only fear, uncertainty, discouragement, and great sorrow. We were not permitted to stand or lie down at will, only when ordered to do so. Police guards watched us scornfully. Because I was a political prisoner they paid close attention to every act. We were forbidden to cry or show any evidence of our anguish. I could only sob out my grievances to myself and shed my tears alone. No one was permitted to visit us or to communicate with us in any way.

I worried about my wife, my parents, my brothers and sisters, my future, and even my life. The more I thought about it, the more frightened and confused I became. Some days I was nearly crazy. My brain would not be quiet, and I could not control my thoughts or my emotions. I felt that I was losing my mind, and I did not know how to prevent it. It seemed to me that I had lost my soul already. From my professional training I knew I was going into prison psychosis and depression.

At that moment, God knew my weakness. He knew that I could not bear my burdens alone. Just in time, one night He showed me a vision. It was clear and powerful.

I saw a light pink curtain a short distance in front of me. It was drawn slowly across my area of vision from left to right. Immediately after the vision disappeared a strong voice came from above to my spirit. The voice said, "See no one but Jesus only."

The vision and the voice awakened me and gave me peace of mind. I remembered the word of Paul, "We are troubled on every side, yet not distressed; we are perplexed, but not in despair; persecuted, but not forsaken; cast down, but not destroyed" (2 Cor. 4:8-9, KJV).

I now knew that I was not alone in the prison. I knew that the Almighty God was with me and beside me. I heard His voice. I felt His presence. He was now teaching and protecting me. That was a spiritual sweetness as sweet as honey. I felt blessed and I could "rejoice in God my Savior" even in prison.

From then on, I was able to shut out depressing thoughts about my family and the future. I could center my thoughts on Jesus only, and I began to recollect the Bible's teachings and its stories one by one. By humming remembered hymn tunes and recalling the words, I learned how to praise God in my darkest and most dangerous times. The Comforter taught me and cheered my heart through unceasing silent communication with Him. Happiness and deep inner comfort flowed through my spirit. Soon my confused mind and vexed heart became calm. Sighing and sadness were replaced by praying and praising. I felt real joy.

The guards and some of the prisoners watching my changed attitudes must have thought that I had no affection for my loved ones. They could not understand why I could be happy. The police often asked me, "Are you so cold-hearted that you never think of the welfare of your wife, your parents, and yourself?"

I just looked at them and did not answer. But in my heart, I knew I really loved my wife and my parents more than my own life. By God's teaching and by His love I had conquered the first big pain—sorrow and terror.

I wished that I could be free, but I had to obey God's command: "See no one but Jesus only." As a soldier of Jesus Christ on the battlefield fighting the devil, I knew that the most important attitude for me was to take up my cross and follow Him. He had said, "He who loves father or mother more than Me is not worthy of Me; and he who loves son or daughter more than Me is not worthy of Me. And he who does not take his cross and follow after Me is not worthy of Me" (Matt. 10:37-38).

I always hummed this song when I felt timid and discouraged:

> *Onward, Christian soldiers! Marching as to war,*
> *With the cross of Jesus Going on before.*
> *Christ, the royal Master, Leads against the foe;*
> *Forward into battle, See, His banners go!*

*Onward, Christian soldiers! Marching as to war,
With the cross of Jesus Going on before.*
—Sabine Baring-Gould

Strengthened in Hunger

The Holy Spirit was teaching me that all we are and all we have has been given to us by God. We must, in turn, place these gifts at His disposal. When we do this, we need not fear whatever we have to meet. We may firmly trust, and rely on Him to lead us. He goes so far as to tell us: "Do not fear those who kill the body, but are unable to kill the soul; but rather fear Him who is able to destroy both soul and body in hell" (Matt. 10:28).

We were given food twice a day and a little drinking water. The portions were small and the food was of poor quality, hence the prisoners were soon near starvation. In spite of short rations we were given heavy work. We were assigned to tear off rubber from old rubberized fabrics. This recycled material was refined and used in a rubber factory. The fees paid for our labor went to the police.

The Red Guards had a motto: "Through labor you will be reformed. It is beneficial to every criminal. This is the only way to lead a man to be a good man." This hard physical and emotional pressure was applied to get the prisoners to confess to the crimes with which they had been charged. Often prisoners made false confessions to escape their anguish. They did not ask, "Is it right or wrong to make a false confession?" Under the pressure they only considered how quickly they could confess to a crime and ask for a lighter sentence. Also you could get the government's favor by reporting crimes of others—whether true or false. The prisoners often reported political misdeeds of neighbors, friends, and even relatives, thus many additional persons were put into prison.

In prison I saw a clear difference between believers

and unbelievers. Although some unbelievers could bear the loss of material possessions, they simply could not bear harm to their physical bodies. They were guided by Satan's philosophy: "Skin for skin! Yes, all that a man has he will give for his life" (Job 2:4). They would think up anything to preserve their bodies from pain—even if they surrendered their morality and lost their souls. To unbelievers the things that are seen and felt seem much more important than the things that are unseen. Almost no unbeliever could keep himself from surrendering to dishonesty when faced with starvation. For nearly three years in jail I watched thousands of prisoners come and go. Some were real criminals; some were political dissenters. I did not find anyone who could stand starvation except Christians who got strength from above.

I faced the same powerful temptation. After three months in prison I could not in myself stand firmly against hunger. I cried to God to save me from lying about myself or incriminating others. I asked Him to get me out of prison. He answered my prayer by giving me this word of guidance: "MAN SHALL NOT LIVE ON BREAD ALONE, BUT ON EVERY WORD THAT PROCEEDS OUT OF THE MOUTH OF GOD" (Matt. 4:4).

I remembered that hunger was the first temptation that Jesus met. Until I myself was hungry I could not understand why the devil first attacked Jesus with starvation. After 40 days in the wilderness without food and water, the devil put on the pressure: "If You are the Son of God, command that these stones become bread" (Matt. 4:3).

I remembered that our Master had won out over this strong attack from the devil. Therefore I, as His disciple, should learn from Him. I asked God to help me triumph over my desperate hunger. I repeated again and again the precious verse, "MAN SHALL NOT LIVE ON BREAD ALONE, BUT ON EVERY WORD THAT PROCEEDS OUT OF THE MOUTH OF

God." Something wonderful happened. Though my body was still starving, I felt no severe hunger pain for nearly three years. Now I understood more clearly what Jesus meant: "The Spirit gives life; the flesh counts for nothing" (John 6:63, NIV).

The police often came and stood in front of the jail door observing me. I think they marvelled at my body bearing up under starvation for such a long time. The prisoners commented to each other, "He was a doctor. Maybe he took good care of himself, or probably he ate specially nourishing food so he has been able to endure more than we."

In my own heart I thanked God for His power and for His Word. I could take no credit for my physical condition or for my peace of mind. I remembered what the Chinese philosopher Mencius said: "Thus when Heaven is about to confer a great office on any man, it first exercises his mind with suffering, and his sinews and bones with toil. It exposes his body to hunger and subjects him to extreme poverty. It confounds his understanding. By all these methods it stimulates his mind, hardens his nature and makes up for his incompetences."

About this time I watched a Christian man who was in the same prison cell. I followed the practice of thanking God secretly for my food, but this man closed his eyes and prayed openly before every meal. Quickly other prisoners took note of it and, to gain favor with the police, some of them reported the man's Christian practice to the guards. With permission from the guards, the prisoners began to beat him and often took away his meal. For the sake of praying openly he was willing to give up a whole day's ration. Like Daniel, this man never gave up praying publicly to avoid spying and persecution. When he missed his food for the day, he did not seem to feel hungry; it made the guards wonder about him.

In order to put more pressure on this Christian to stop his public mealtime prayers, the guards cuffed his hands so tightly behind his back that the pain could be endured for only a few minutes. He soon cried loudly, tears on his cheeks: "Lord, Savior, save me!"

The unbelievers laughed at him, but they watched his confidence and piety with much curiosity. I was not as courageous as he, but I sympathized with him and asked God to save this faithful Christian who glorified Him by accepting such punishment for his faith.

One day the guard came to the jail, called this man's number, and said loudly, "You are a simple and pure Christian, but foolish and stubborn. Now you are going to be released. Your mother is waiting for you outside the door. You should wake up from your superstition. How perfect you would be, if you did not believe in your Jesus."

The prisoners did not agree with the guards. They whispered cautiously to each other, "He really is a good man; he is like Jesus—so single-minded and steadfast."

I thanked God for his release, and for his good deeds; and I praised God for our Lord's name being glorified by this man's courage and Christian witness. Punishment and starvation could not stop his relationship with Christ nor quiet his powerful testimony. Hallelujah!

When I watched him suffer so bitterly, I supposed that someday I also would be treated this way.

"Can I stand as firmly as he does?" I asked myself. My answer was, "No. Not in my own strength." There is no man who does not love his own comfort. I thought of Simon Peter who tried to stand firmly by himself but three times denied Jesus instead of confessing Him boldly.

I could not imagine what I would do if put under such severe punishment. Would I deny Jesus, and betray those who were innocent? God forbid! I asked Christ to give me strength every day. If I should be confronted by a cross, I prayed: "Let me keep my soul clean, rather than surrender to the flesh or anything that belongs to it."

Prepared for Persecution

One night about three months after I was arrested, I heard a voice coming to my spirit asking me, "Do you love Me?"

I knew it was the voice of the Lord. Once He had asked Peter the same question. Now He was speaking to me.

At that time my spirit was full of sorrow. I knew there were times in my life when I had failed. Sometimes it was thoughtlessness or failure to pray. I cried bitterly, shedding uncontrolled tears. Shamefully and regretfully I replied, "Lord, I love You! Lord . . . Lord . . . I love You, but not enough . . . not enough . . . not enough."

When I woke up my tears were still flowing, and I was in great sadness. I thought, what was the use to offer Him more love here in the prison? Why had I not loved Him more before persecution came? There in the darkness I rebuked myself for some time.

Who could know that the next morning I would be called out for trial? God knew.

It was cloudy, cold, and windy. In a small dark room about 20 people stood around me. The door and the windows were shut, and there was no artificial light. I wondered why so many people were there for the inquiry. One man asked me fiercely, "Will you be faithful to us?"

"I will," I answered.

Another said, "If so, tell us all you know."

I answered, "I have committed no crime. I have already told you about my life and my work."

Before the answer was finished a policeman gave me heavy blows on both ears, and said, "We know that you are not willing to tell us how bad you are. But the facts are in the file. There is enough evidence to prove that you are an important member of the counterrevolutionary clique." Then they started to fist me and kick me from my head to my feet. I was numbed by their beating. One of them shouted loudly, "Shoot him. If you do not confess, double punishment will be given to you."

I answered nothing but simply committed my soul to God and endured all that I could. After a little while one said, "Do not fool with such an evil person. Cuff him."

Another spoke up, "Not answering will not diminish your crimes. Your silence shows that you continue to stubbornly insist on your reactionary stand."

Then they cuffed my hands behind my back tightly, saying:

"We will not take off your iron cuffs until you reveal to us everything that you have done, and until you indict others for their crimes. You may be silent, but the cuffs will make you speak. Steel is more stubborn than you. Get back to jail and consider your crimes deeply. If you are willing to tell us the truth without reservation, our arms are outstretched to welcome you to the proletarian class. If you do not confess, you will receive punishment for what you have done against the Chinese people."

When I went back to jail, the guards warned all the prisoners, "This is a case of political crime. A bad man deserves his punishment because he is not willing to confess his evil doings."

The prisoners were surprised because we had lived together for three months and they had not seen in me any sign of antigovernment activity.

When the next meal came, I was hungry. All day I had been without food and water. But how could I feed myself with my hands cuffed behind my back? Another prisoner saw my need and began to feed me with a spoon. When the guard saw him helping me, he shouted: "Stand up.

Who told you to feed him? Are you siding with him against our government? If you feed him again, you will be handcuffed also. Let him do everything for himself. Let him eat like a dog."

The food was dumped on the floor in front of me. I could only lick at it and smear my face, but I believed that God knew where I was and what I needed.

The handcuffs were made so that they tightened automatically if you moved your hands even a little. After several hours my shoulder joints and wrists became extremely painful. My hands were swollen until they could not move inside the steel cuffs. During the day the police forced me to sit upright in this painful position, rather than bending my back or lying on my side on the floor. The guard said, "This will give you a good taste of an iron fist. Why don't you surrender and confess? Remember the teaching of our Red Sun and of our Chairman Mao and Vice-chairman Lin: 'Surrender your arms, or we will shoot.'"

But I had no firearms, no weapon at all; only a clear conscience and a will to do right.

That night I could not sleep or turn my body. In the darkness I cried quietly, because showing emotion due to pain was forbidden in the prison. I shed my silent tears and prayed for God to deliver me from these evil men. I remembered that even the great prophet Elijah had requested that he might die. Was I stronger than he? No. So, I prayed with him: "It is enough; now, O Lord, take away my life" (1 Kings 19:4, KJV).

But a saving memory stirred in my mind. I recalled Christ's question to me only the night before, "Do you love Me?"

Only hours earlier, I had been awakened by my sorrowful confession, "I love You . . . but not enough . . . not enough . . . not enough."

Then I pled, "God, give me strength to suffer all that is necessary, but command them to take off my cuffs."

The next day I still had my hands cuffed behind my back. But the pain was eased when I remembered His love for me. I hummed a hymn that I had often sung without grasping its truth:

> *The cross that He gave may be heavy,*
> *But it ne'er outweighs His grace.*
> *The storm that I feared may surround me,*
> *But it ne'er excludes His face.*
>
> *The cross is not greater than His grace.*
> *The storm cannot hide His blessed face.*
> *I am satisfied to know*
> *That, with Jesus, here below*
> *I can conquer every foe.*
>
> *The thorns in my path are not sharper*
> *Than composed His crown for me;*
> *The cup that I drink, not more bitter*
> *Than He drank in Gethsemane.*
>
> —Ballington Booth

Without this ministry to my spirit I would have gone crazy. The pain was more than a human being could bear. Knowing the words of the Bible is one thing, but experiencing a cross of pain is very different.

For two days and nights I suffered. Then on the morning of the third day, the police called me out for inquiry again. They took off my cuffs, saying, "Have you tasted our iron fists long enough? Will you still resist? We hope you will be wiser now. You should know that we will be satisfied only if you confess all that you know. If you continue to refuse, we will cuff you again—this time for two weeks. Back to the jail; write down all your crimes as soon as possible."

I knew that I was falsely charged with crime. I could

not confess an untruth and tell a lie even to escape further punishment. I committed myself completely to God and wrote the same true answers that I had given before. The police did not follow through on their threats, and I praised God for revealing himself to me in time to give me the strength that I needed. I knew a deep sense of joy because He had given me the strength to resist this evil pressure. The power of His words was stronger than the iron chain. My soul rejoiced in God my Savior as He gave me a personal assurance of the reality of Psalm 1:

> Blessed is the man that walketh not in the counsel of the ungodly, nor standeth in the way of sinners, nor sitteth in the seat of the scornful.
> But his delight is in the law of the Lord; and in his law doth he meditate day and night.
> And he shall be like a tree planted by the rivers of water, that bringeth forth his fruit in his season; his leaf also shall not wither; and whatsoever he doeth shall prosper. . . .
> For the Lord knoweth the way of the righteous: but the way of the ungodly shall perish *(Ps. 1:1-3, 6, KJV).*

Chapter 4

Deepening Persecution

In prison, although I forced myself not to think of my wife, I always prayed for her peace and safety. I also asked God to bring us together again. I promised Him that if we could meet and live together, we would not live for ourselves, but only for Him.

A Sustaining Vision

One night I had another prison vision. I saw my wife wearing a dark red skirt with a white short-sleeved blouse. She was smiling and coming toward me through a wide gate in the garden wall. Over the gate I saw a large sign: VILLAGE OF FAITH AND RIGHTEOUSNESS. Just in front of the gate was a beautiful flower bed with some boys and girls playing nearby. The air was quiet and I could almost smell the fragrance of the flowers. I watched her coming closer and closer. Then the vision faded. I awakened sad but also happy. I was sad to be shut up in prison but happy because God had showed me that we could meet again in the Village of Faith and Righteousness.

These two words, *faith* and *righteousness,* became my guiding lights while in prison. I understood as never before that I could not with my own mind and strength choose the words that I was to think, or speak, or write. All must come from God. Without faith and righteousness I could not trust Him for my life and my deliverance. The way of faith is narrow—but it leads to life.

"Faith is the assurance of things hoped for, the conviction of things not seen.... Without faith it is impossible to please Him, for he who comes to God must believe that He is, and that He is a rewarder of those who seek Him.... By faith [men of old] conquered kingdoms, performed acts of righteousness, obtained promises, shut the mouths of lions, quenched the power of fire, escaped the edge of the sword, from weakness were made strong, became mighty in war, put foreign armies to flight" (Heb. 11:1, 6, 33-34).

I thank God that He occasionally gave me His vision and His voice to guide me while I was in the very pit. There was no one else to help me, not even a little bit. But the Holy Spirit is the Teacher whom Jesus sent. He taught me what I needed to know. Thanks be to God.

Do Not Be Anxious

Jesus taught His disciples: "When they arrest you and deliver you up, do not be anxious beforehand about what you are to say, but say whatever is given you in that hour; for it is not you who speak, but it is the Holy Spirit" (Mark 13:11). This promise was often fulfilled literally for me in the prison.

At the time of Lin Piao they used a quotation from Mao: "Class Struggle is the Staff." The staff is the key link in any situation. They used this class struggle to stir up strife and fighting everywhere. Education stopped. Factories closed. Transportation shut down all over the country. Hospitals were closed. The only activity that never stopped was the class struggle—conflict over a social theory. There was no morality, no charity, no kindness, no love, no reality. It brought the country to the brink of total collapse.

The prisons were not immune from this social poison. The police said, "The prison is the focus of class struggle." So they forced everyone to accuse each other. They said, "It is the life of our party. If we stop the struggle, we will be killed by the bourgeois class. If you do not struggle against them, they will put us to death. You must follow Mao's teaching. Put it into action. Let us fight—struggle without stopping until victory is completely won in every field by the proletarian class. We must struggle not only to force everyone to conform but also to accept proletarian ideology."

Every prisoner was highly pressured to follow these guidelines by accusing others—the more the better. In order to please the police and gain favor for themselves, most of the prisoners wrote down anything they had seen or heard from others.

Many innocent people were tortured, or put into prison. Accused prisoners were taken out for severe questioning and punishment. Under this system China's people came to fear and to hate each other.

One night I heard a voice in my spirit. It was a revelation from God to me: "This class struggle is self-destructive. It can finally lead only to death."

I understood that such immoral strife was an evil next to death itself. I could not follow this path. If I did so, I would forfeit my morality and lose my soul.

When others followed the line, I kept silent. It thus appeared that I was against Lin's teaching—and it was a crime not to obey his word. They could charge me with criminal offence and sentence me to death for it.

Forgive Your Enemies

In the face of this danger, Jesus' teaching was etched deeply into my spirit: "Whoever wishes to save his life shall lose it; but whoever loses his life for My sake shall find it. For what will a man be profited, if he gains the whole world, and forfeits his soul? Or what will a man give in exchange for his soul?" (Matt. 16:25-26).

The Holy Spirit helped me resolve to obey my Master's

call rather than to follow the popular path. Praise the Lord, He led me in paths of peace!

What should I do when people speak falsely against me? The Holy Spirit reminded me of the words of Jesus: "I say to you, love your enemies, and pray for those who persecute you in order that you may be sons of your Father who is in heaven" (Matt. 5:44-45). Jesus also reminded me of His instructions to Peter in the Garden of Gethsemane: "Put away your sword." Sometimes I felt that humanly I had good reasons at least to defend myself, but Jesus said to me just as clearly as He said to Peter: "Keep your sword in its sheath." He helped me to obey His Word, although more often than not it seemed unreasonable to me.

I was convinced in my mind that His way was higher than my way, and His thinking was better than my thinking—but I couldn't feel it. The Holy Spirit really helped me to accept Jesus' way instead of following my own ideas. I was like a child obeying God's Word. Gradually He showed me that such careful obedience is the way we are to live in His kingdom; it is the way we become like our Lord and Master. He took me through "the valley of the shadow of death." By His help He enabled me to conquer my fear of the evils around me. He saved me from the stain of unchristian resentment and retaliation. But I confess, my most difficult spiritual lesson was learning not to fight back against persecution—the persecution that came to me because I could not take part in the destructive class struggle.

God seemed to vindicate me when suddenly the man who had lied against me lost his mind. All of his false accusations to the police were canceled because of his madness.

Signs of the Times

The Bible gives some indications of the last days. The disciples asked, "What will be the sign of Your coming, and of the end of the age?" Jesus answered them, "See to it that no one misleads you. . . . Then they will deliver you up to tribulation, and will kill you, and you will be hated by all nations on account of My name. At that time many will fall away and will deliver up one another and hate one another. . . . And because lawlessness is increased, most people's love will grow cold. But the one who endures to the end, it is he who shall be saved" (Matt. 24:3-4, 9-10, 12-13).

These words are an accurate description of what happened in China during the Cultural Revolution. Because men betrayed one another, they hated each other. This was a direct result of the following practices and teachings of the class struggle.

They liked to use nice-sounding phrases to conceal evil practices.

> Betraying one another was called "Helping you to realize your mistakes."
>
> Encouraging children to rebel against their families was called "Saving parents from sliding into the deep pit of the bourgeois class."
>
> Obeying the Red Guards' commands and all their orders was represented as "Loving and being faithful to your country."
>
> Sacrificing yourself to provide luxury for leaders was represented as "Dedicating yourself to Communism."
>
> For attractive young women to give their bodies to amuse or to be ravished by Red Guards in authority was called "Offering your youth for your motherland."
>
> Persecuting you more intensely was called "Liberating you from your bondage."
>
> Doing more work for little or no payment was designated "Serving your people."

Such dishonesty is condemned by God's Word, which warns: "Woe to those who call evil good, and good evil;

who substitute darkness for light and light for darkness; who substitute bitter for sweet, and sweet for bitter!" (Isa. 5:20).

Suffering for Christ

In this ideological class struggle many preachers and Christian laymen were sentenced to long prison terms. Some were forced to work on labor farms. Others were shot. Churches were taken away and turned to other uses; they became secular meeting places, manufacturing plants, or cattle barns.

One Christian sister, just after the birth of her son, was sentenced to prison for seven years because of her faith. When released from prison, she was not permitted to go back home, even though her father-in-law was dying of cancer and wished to see her once again. She was sent away to a farm for heavy labor.

At her departure, her own parents cried but she consoled them through her tears, "Do not be dismayed or dejected. Every cup from above, even if bitter is also good. Christians should share Christ's pain and suffering as well as His grace and favor." After the downfall of the Gang of Four she was vindicated by the police and permitted to return home.

Another Christian sister met similar persecution for the sake of Jesus. She, her parents, and her husband were all arrested on the same day. She was forced to renounce her family and was given hard work in the fields. One morning in the autumn as she swept up fallen leaves she felt deeply depressed. Why had God done this to her and her family? Had they sinned against God? Were they worse than their evil oppressors? Was God just to do this to His children? Through her tears, question after question tumbled from her tortured mind.

Under such oppression, China's Christians could only join with earlier children of God:

O God, why hast Thou rejected us forever?
Why does Thine anger smoke against the sheep
of Thy pasture?
Remember Thy congregation, which Thou hast
purchased of old,
Which Thou hast redeemed to be the tribe
of Thine inheritance . . .
. . . Let not the oppressed return dishonored;
Let the afflicted and needy praise Thy name.
Do arise, O God, and plead Thine own cause
(Ps. 74:1-2, 21-22).

Thank God, He hears the cry of His persecuted people. This Chinese child of God paused in her work and lifted her eyes to heaven for an answer. Suddenly she saw the heavens opened and a voice came to her through the clouds, "Do not be in great sorrow, I am always with you."

She was greatly comforted and found strength to endure for more than 10 years. Eventually in 1979, her whole family was vindicated and released.

Our hearts can sing: "Gracious is the Lord, and righteous; yes, our God is compassionate. The Lord preserves the simple; I was brought low, and He saved me. Return to your rest, O my soul, for the Lord has dealt bountifully with you. For Thou hast rescued my soul from death, my eyes from tears, my feet from stumbling" (Ps. 116:5-8).

A New Plot

Confucius said, "The progress of the superior man is upwards; the progress of the mean man is downwards." My captors, having failed in their rough and wild ways, thought up a tricky plot. Offering a beautiful girl to a hero or to a strong opponent is a famous plot in Chinese history. It is called the Beautiful Girl Plot. I did not know about the police plans, but the living and omniscient God knew them—and He prepared me.

One night after about six months in the prison I was given another vision. A crowd of young ladies appeared before me; their arms were linked together, their heads and bodies swaying gracefully. They formed a half circle around me. At that moment I heard a voice say, "They behave this way, not to save you; instead, they want you to stay in prison forever."

I marveled at this wisdom, but I could not understand what it meant. Early the next morning, March 8, 1969, the police came to the jail. They opened the door, called my number, and ordered me out. My hands were again cuffed behind my back and I was put into a jeep. As we drove through the streets they told me nothing, but I feared I was being taken to be sentenced to many more years in prison—or even to be shot. All I could do was to ask God's mercy and deliverance.

After a ride of about 15 minutes, the jeep stopped and I was led into a large building that I did not recognize. As we entered, they told me that this was a class struggle meeting. I must confess everything that they had charged me with and reveal everything I knew.

Class struggle! How obnoxious the words were to me! In the old dynasty, the authorities caught two slaves and gave them swords, put them in an arena, and forced them to fight each other until one was killed. If they did not want to fight, both would be put to death. On the stage the authorities drank wine and amused themselves watching the slaves kill each other. The time of slaves in China was long gone, but these authorities used other tortures in the 20th century.

The room was full of spectators. As I entered they began shouting, "Down with the rebel. Down with the running dog of the bourgeois class. Down with the children who cling to the bourgeois families. Long live the Cultural Revolution. Resistance leads only to death. We will not kill you if you surrender."

My hands were cuffed behind my back, and the guards pushed my head and shoulders down close to the floor. Then they pulled my head up by my hair showing my face to the crowd.

"This is a good lesson to teach every one of you," they shouted. "He is rebellious against us. He must be sentenced if he does not change his stand today. Everyone here will bear testimony to his crime. Down with the crumbs of bourgeois class. It is right to rebel against the bourgeois and their belongings. Making revolution is no crime."

I knew that I had not committed any crime against the law. On the contrary, they had broken the law by detaining me without a just cause. The power was in their hands temporarily, but I believed it would show the glory of God if I stood firmly. When I said nothing, it made them angry. Unknown to me, my brothers were being held in separate cells just off from this court room. At this point the police dragged them from their cells to confront me. The authorities intended to strike down our whole family, but God was on our side. That morning they harassed and threatened all of us, but they could not get anything they wished to know from any of us. At the end of the morning I was warned that my attitude and behavior in the class struggle session was a crime. I was then dragged out in front of the spectators.

In the afternoon they brought me into a smaller room on the second floor. They removed my handcuffs and ordered me to sit down at the head of a rectangular table. I wondered why the police had removed the cuffs when I had resisted them so steadfastly. For lunch they gave me a small amount of rice with a few bean sprouts—nothing else, not even a cup of water. But they said, "We are giving you a better lunch here than in the prison. You'll know how kind we are." While I was eating, a number of young ladies came into the room. They all sat down around the table and smiled in a friendly manner. They then inquired, "Have you finished your lunch? After lunch we will have a discussion; you may tell us what you learned from this morning's questioning."

I could not understand their behavior, smiling at me as if they were kind and friendly. In a low, gentle voice one of them pled with me, "You are the youngest one in your family. We wish to save you first; to help you out from the dirty pit of the bourgeois class. We can save you and set you free, but only if you really change your stand and come over to our side. We want you to change. You are clever, because you have graduated from the university. We hope you will also be clever in politics."

Then another said, "It is pitiful to bury your whole life in the pit of the bourgeois class. We do not wish to punish you but to instruct and save you. If you tell us the things that you know without any reservations, it will show that you are deciding to break relations with the bourgeois. If your testimony satisfies us, we promise to set you free after the meeting."

A third young woman picked up the appeal, "We know your whole family and your friends. We have not detained your parents, although they have a history of opposition to our proletarian class. Your parents and your wife are worrying about you. If you are set free this afternoon, you may go back immediately to be with your family."

The fourth girl concluded, "You were married only five days, were you not? We know how hard it must be for you to be in prison. Now is your best chance for release."

At that moment I remembered the vision that God

had given me the night before. I recognized that these young women were helping the police, trying to seduce me into saying what the police wanted me to say. They would have succeeded if God in His providence had not forewarned me. He had told me clearly, "They behave this way, not to save you; instead, they want you to stay in prison forever."

Months later after my release, my wife told me that at that time she was not at home. The girls knew that the authorities were searching for her to arrest her also. The girls were lying to me.

From this point on, I was respectful toward the young women—but unyielding. After two more hours of guile, they changed their attitudes. Pounding the table, they shouted wildly, "You stubborn fool. You are doomed to be sentenced. You should be shot. Put the cuffs on. Back to jail. You do not know what is good for you. Stay in prison until you die. You are a rotten troublemaker to resist the control of our proletarian class. We should kill you!"

I now knew their undisguised attitudes and their real purpose. I stretched out my hands to be cuffed and went back to the jail knowing that they were very angry with me. I feared they would give me even greater punishment. I could not cry aloud and was not permitted to sob, but I cried deeply in my heart, asking God to deliver me from their evil intention and power. As I prayed, a hymn came quietly but powerfully to my mind. I hummed the music again and again. My sadness and fright were gone. The words I recalled were:

> *Never a trial that He is not there,*
> *Never a burden that He doth not bear,*
> *Never a sorrow that He doth not share;*
> *Moment by moment, I'm under His care.*

With my fears gone, I remembered Jesus' words: "Blessed are the meek; for they shall inherit the earth" (Matt. 5:5, KJV). Atrocity and ferocity cannot finally triumph, though temporarily they may be successful. I recalled the first vision that God gave me. I was sure that the vice-chairman, Lin Piao, the evil Gang of Four, and all who sided with them would eventually go down. The devil was temporarily frustrating God's purpose for my life, but I believed that God would use me someday as His witness and for His glory.

In our Christian walk, often "we are afflicted in every way, but not crushed; perplexed, but not despairing; persecuted, but not forsaken; struck down, but not destroyed; always carrying about in the body the dying of Jesus, that the life of Jesus also may be manifested in our body" (2 Cor. 4:8-10). I thanked God for His Word that had lighted my pathway and guided me.

From the spiritual point of view, I realized that every evil thing that had happened to me was inspired by the devil, even though carried out by evil men. I knew this was a spiritual war against the devil, so I could not fight in my own wisdom or in my purely human way. If I did so, I would be defeated by Satan. There was only one way to overcome: by trusting and obeying Christ fully.

One precious verse of Scripture always admonished me at this point: "Therefore let him who thinks he stands take heed lest he fall" (1 Cor. 10:12). The Bible teaches us, "Though we walk in the flesh, we do not war according to the flesh, for the weapons of our warfare are not of the flesh, but divinely powerful for the destruction of fortresses. We are destroying speculations and every lofty thing raised up against the knowledge of God, and we are taking every thought captive to the obedience of Christ" (2 Cor. 10:3-5).

Chapter 5

Ignored and Attacked Again

Something wonderful happened after this severe conflict and spiritual victory. I was held in the prison undisturbed for many months, except for being moved to Cell No. 7, a room for political prisoners. There was no questioning. Every day I tried to follow the teaching, "See no one but Jesus only." I prayed silently, hummed hymns very softly, and recalled the Bible verses that I could remember. At that time I fully experienced that God's Word was my life. How hungry I was for His truth! How much I desired to have a Bible to read! Communication with God through prayer and singing hymns was my spiritual breath; but both had to be as silent as breathing.

A New Police Officer

Then one night I saw another vision. The frowning chief of police had on his winter cap. It was tilted to one side, and he was smoking. The white smoke rings showed clearly against the blue sky. As I was wondering what it meant, a voice said, "He is dry of plots and exhausted of wisdom."

I praised God for His revelation to me. Subsequent events proved the vision to be true. After several weeks another young policeman about 25 years of age came to question me. He said, "From now on I am in charge of your case. The former officer has left for other work. I hope that you will be honest with me. I will not cuff you or beat you any more. I wish you would cooperate with me so we can work out your case as quickly as possible. You have been under arrest for more than a year. Why do you admit your crimes only as slowly as squeezing toothpaste from a tube? The Chinese People's Government never wishes to destroy a criminal. We hope to help him improve. We try to encourage a good attitude toward us by your being honest and confessing quickly. But serious punishment will follow obstinate resistance. Do you understand our policy?"

I had never seen this young policeman before, and I did not know anything about his sincerity. But he sounded more reasonable than the former one, and I liked his words, "I will not cuff you. I will not beat you. I want you to cooperate with me to work out your case as quickly as possible."

Were these good words from his conscience or just from his lips? I did not know. We Chinese have two proverbs: "Knowing one's face is different from knowing his heart," and "You can draw a picture of a tiger's skin, but you cannot show his bones."

I did not know how to deal with him, so I breathed a prayer asking God to guide me and to protect me. Then I told him all the facts again. I concluded: "I have not committed any crime against the law."

One night a little later, God showed me a vision of this policeman. He was crouched low, sneaking like a thief through the gate of our jail yard. His cap was pulled down, covering nearly half of his face. After the vision disappeared, a voice spoke to my spirit, "Nothing can be found outside; now he is secretly searching to find proofs from your fellow prisoners for the charges against you."

Then I knew that this policeman was following the same plan as the former one. He had only changed his tactics with me; his goals were the same. The Gang of Four were throwing people into prison just to achieve their political goals. They wished to seize power, to change the government policies to satisfy their personal views. Political tests were made on suspected opponents, just as we had made chemical tests of inanimate materials in the science laboratory.

Persons suspected of divergent views were quickly arrested, tortured, and pressed to write down where they disagreed with the new policies. With those written statements in hand, the Red Guard could prove that their suspicions were true. With this evidence they could send the victim to prison, thus sweeping away those who did not agree with their evil ways.

For fear of saying something that would be used against me, from that day on I scarcely said a word to the prisoners around me. After two months I was moved to room No. 3; then in two more weeks, they sent me to No. 4. It was only about 7 by 10 feet. There were so many of us in this small room that we could hardly all sit down on the floor at the same time during the day; and there was barely room for us to lie on the floor at night. I could not sleep as well as some of the others because of poor health after being detained for nearly 18 months. I was so emaciated that my bones showed prominently. I was short of breath because the room was too overcrowded and there was only one small window near the ceiling.

By the dim electric light through the steel grid door, I could see that there were many bugs on the walls. All night they crawled up and down. One night I could not sleep. Thinking to help all of us by killing the bugs, I swatted them against the wall. I killed at least 200 during the night, not thinking that they would leave bloody stains on the walls. The guards were terribly angry when they saw the stains. They were more concerned with the appearance of the walls than with the comfort of the men. One of the guards demanded angrily, "Why did you stain the walls with blood? Are you challenging us? You are to clean the walls and then stand erect all day until you recognize your fault."

My feet were swollen and my legs so weak that I could hardly stand an hour. But stand all day I must. It was an order and I was being punished. There were no basic human rights for prisoners at that time.

At one o'clock one afternoon, without warning, an accusation meeting was called in our prison. Two officers came to my room and ordered me to stand in front of all the other prisoners. Once again the guards cuffed my hands behind me and pushed my head down. I thought it was an unauthorized cuffing by the local guards because I remembered the young police officer had promised me, "I will not cuff you. I will not beat you."

The head guard said: "We who have come today to conduct this meeting have never been here before. But this stubborn one has been standing against our government for a long time. He has not only done many evils outside the prison, but he has often broken the rules of the jail. He refuses to be instructed and reformed."

He then gave me such a heavy blow on my face that it staggered me. I saw lights flashing in my eyes and heard a loud buzzing in my ears. The guard then exclaimed, "How poisonous he is! To you prisoners he has the look of an intellectual, gentle and serious. But he is more poisonous than a viper. Do not be deceived by him. Think back and tell us all that he has done or spoken in this room. We already have proof of his crimes in our files. He stops at nothing. We will show all of you his final sentence." These same accusations and orders were given to the prisoners in all the cells where I had been held.

In order to please the guards, the prisoners one by one made charges against me. It lasted for five hours. My knees trembled partly from weakness—but partly from fear because I was only human. I imagined that I would soon be sentenced—maybe shot.

At 8 p.m. the head guard called me to his office room and told me in a solemn voice, "We are always strict if you stick to your wrong point of view, but we welcome anyone who is willing to be converted. Now I am going to take off your cuffs and give you one more opportunity to repent. Go back to your room and write down what you should. We will not always be patiently waiting for your confession. You will be in contempt of our government and guilty of committing a crime if you continue to resist confessing your misdeeds. Your fate depends on your own attitude."

From being tightly bound for seven hours my wrists were swollen and bloody when he took off the cuffs. I went back to my room and there reflected, Really, what crimes have I committed? They have ransacked our home and taken all that we have. They have taken us into custody and kept me in isolation cells. They have broken up our family. All of this they have done outside of the law. Why do they feel no shame for what they have done?

I still believed that truth would win out in the end. I could not follow their theory. I could not walk in their wrong ways just because they had guns in their hands. Christ helped me to hold on to my faith. My spirit was strengthened when I recalled the testimony of the Psalmist:

> The Lord is my light and my salvation; whom shall I fear? The Lord is the defense of my life; whom shall I dread? When evildoers came upon me to devour my flesh, my adversaries and my enemies, they stumbled and fell. Though a host encamp against me, my heart will not fear; though war arise against me, in spite of this I shall be confident. . . . Do not deliver me over to the desire of my adversaries; for false witnesses have risen against me, and such as breathe out violence. I would have despaired unless I had believed that I

would see the goodness of the Lord in the land of the living. Wait for the Lord; be strong, and let your heart take courage; yes, wait for the Lord *(Ps. 27:1-3, 12-14)*.

I wrote not one dishonest word that the guards wished from me.

We Chinese have a saying, "Taking away your life to get your money." It applied to my case at this time. I learned that the accusation meeting in the jail was ordered by the young policeman to cover his dishonesty. When arrested, I had 500 yen in my pocket. The money was put in the bag in my case file. This young police officer secretly took the money because he needed it for his marriage. To cover his theft, he decided to have me sentenced to 15 years in prison. But his charges were rejected by the high court for lack of proof, and he could not raise all of this money to replace it in the file. Hoping to get some significant proofs, he ordered the guards to hold the accusation meeting inside the prison—a thing that was almost never done.

Once again this young policeman demanded that the high court sentence me; this time for seven years. He based his accusations on "proofs" from the prison. Once again the charges were rejected by the court and the policeman was ordered to make certain of his evidence. It was God's blessed love and care that revealed to me the dishonest character of this young policeman when He showed the man to me in my vision as a thief coming through the gate of the jail yard.

Finally the young policeman took my cash and spent it for furniture, but no one knew it at the time because he was the officer in charge of my file. That much stolen money was not enough to satisfy him. Later he was caught stealing public money and was discharged by the police. He then confessed that he had already used up my money.

There is a Chinese proverb, "Evil is recompensed for

evil, and good is recompensed for good. If not recompensed, it will be in time because when the time is up, all must be recompensed."

Deepening Discouragement

In April 1970, my wife was caught and put into the same prison. At the time I did not know about her harassment, flight, or imprisonment. If I had known about her arrest and being in the same prison, I could not have borne the mental anguish. So near and yet so far! God knew my weakness so He did not show it to me. It was His mercy.

From March 1970 to March 1971 I was imprisoned in room Nos. 6, 5, and 9. They moved me from one room to another just to confuse my mind and to keep me from discovering what they were thinking and planning. The guards often put up new accusation boards with threatening words on the wall in front of me. One of them was: "Death shall follow after your stubbornness"; another was, "Bring your granite head to see your God."

Sitting silently from morning until night and sleeping on the rough wooden floor was cruel physical and mental punishment. I often asked myself, "What is my future? Can I ever be set free? Will the government shoot me or give me a serious sentence? How many years of my life will be spent in prison? Am I wrong not to defend myself when they accuse me?"

The questions came because I was really weak in body, and sometimes my faith faltered.

One night God showed me that one of my family members was grumbling against me. He was saying that I should not have left home with my mother when I took her away for medical care. In my dreams, I cried out to him, "Knowing the whole course of events, you are grumbling against me even under these conditions?"

I wept under his criticism. How could he grumble at the unfortunate outcome of my efforts, instead of sympathizing with me and praying for me?

When I finally got home I asked him, "Did you grumble at me after I was arrested?"

He frankly replied, "Yes. I was very angry with you for leaving our native home. Then I saw you in the class struggle meeting when we were forced to stand before the crowd and the accusers. Your face was as pale and white as paper. I felt there was no hope for you to be set free. Because of your stand, these evil men were determined to put you under sentence. They were like roaring lions devastating and devouring our whole family." In that honest moment between brothers, love and forgiveness healed our wounds.

Some days in prison were especially filled with torment, uncertainty, and despair. I was often depressed, and it was hard to get my spirit up. Special days in our family had come and gone—birthdays, wedding anniversaries, holidays. These were days of bleak remembrance and dashed hopes. No letters could be mailed or received. I had not had a bath for a year and a half since I had been taken into custody, and I did not get to go outdoors except for questioning.

I told God that I could not wait any longer because I was sick. My body was beginning to swell and my belly was distended by fluids in the tissues. I could not stand because of weakness. I often sighed and, with Job, asked God impatiently, "Why do the wicked still live, continue on, also become very powerful? Their descendants are established with them in their sight, and their offspring before their eyes, their houses are safe from fear, neither is the rod of God on them. . . . They spend their days in prosperity" (Job 21:7-9,13).

I felt that my life would soon end. It was also the time

when my faith was tested to see whether I would be faithful to Christ even to death. Many things I did not understand. But I knew that my Redeemer lived, and at the last He would take His stand on the earth.

During the time of my imprisonment I was not always strong. Sometimes I was very weak in spirit. But when I saw Jesus, then I saw no one else—not my loved ones, nor the wicked; not even my very sick self. At those times I did not see the distresses around me. I could say to my sagging spirit: "Why are you in despair, O my soul? And why are you disturbed within me? Hope in God, for I shall again praise Him, the help of my countenance, and my God" (Ps. 43:5).

I often hummed a special hymn to clear my mind of fret, impatience, and despair:

> *All the way my Saviour leads me.*
> *What have I to ask beside?*
> *Can I doubt His tender mercy*
> *Who thro' life has been my Guide?*
> *Heav'nly peace, divinest comfort,*
> *Here by faith in Him to dwell!*
> *For I know whate'er befall me,*
> *Jesus doeth all things well.*
> —Fanny J. Crosby

Another hymn also consoled me very often:

> *Jesus is all the world to me:*
> *My Life, my Joy, my All.*
> *He is my Strength from day to day;*
> *Without Him I would fall.*
> *When I am sad, to Him I go;*
> *No other one can cheer me so.*
> *When I am sad, He makes me glad.*
> *He's my Friend.*
> —Will L. Thompson

On the face of my small sewing bag, I made a cross with black and blue threads; it would be a good reminder for me to fight with the devil even unto death. I recalled the scripture, "It is good that he waits silently for the salvation of the Lord. It is good for a man that he should bear the yoke in his youth. Let him sit alone and be silent since He has laid it on him" (Lam. 3:26-28). I tried to wait patiently for deliverance, because I knew that God's promise was to the one who endured to the end; he it was who should be saved.

One night I was caught up into heaven. I clearly knew that my body was still in the jail, but my spirit was in a very beautiful and large garden. It was neat and clean; not a single leaf on the ground. The sunshine felt warm and comfortable. The sky was light blue, and the garden was full of tall pines and other evergreen trees. This was heaven. An old man wearing a pure white robe guided me through the garden showing me its beauty. I begged him, "Please let me stay here, just to lie under the trees. Even a small place here is better than suffering in the prison down on the earth."

The old man smiled and told me kindly, "No, you cannot stay here now. You will go back to your parents and serve them."

Then I felt myself moving downward. I wakened from my vision with great comfort and peace. It felt like my face was shining, but there was no mirror in which I could see myself. The other prisoners commented, "His complexion is so good. Look! His face is bright. Why are you so happy today, Old Lagger?"

That was my nickname that they called me in the prison instead of using my prisoner number. I was "Old Lagger" because I was the one who had been imprisoned so long without a final sentence. They asked me, "Do you think the longer you stay in prison the happier you will be?"

I did not tell them what had happened to me. I just thanked God for His wonderful promise. From that day I knew for certain that I would be set free. This was about one year before I was released.

Chapter 6

Life in a Prison Hospital

My mother had been ordered back to our native town, and she went there by train two weeks after I had been arrested. She met my father at our house, which had become a ruin of brick and mud. Only the frame stood intact. But they grieved more because their three sons were in the custody of the police.

Pressures at Home

My mother and father tried to build life again under these frightening circumstances. They were allowed only 10 yen per month by the Red Guards. I thank God that my parents, even in these difficult conditions, still tithed to help other Christians who were suffering more than themselves.

Although my parents were not put into prison, their hearts were broken. With their children in prison and their life savings gone, they said that without Jesus they would have ended their own lives. Everyone could harass them. Even very young children mocked them. Most close relatives were far away, and some spoke evil against them. Former friends rejected them, saying, "This is God's justice and punishment to your home because of your sins."

One old Christian, however, gave my parents encouragement. When he was sick God talked to him about my father and mother. After praying for them, he told his grandchildren, "This family is like Job's family. We must not despise them, even though so many people are speaking evil against them. God will bless this family more and more. Go tell them of this promise: 'He has not despised nor abhorred the affliction of the afflicted; neither has He hidden His face from him; but when he cried to Him for help, He heard' (Ps. 22:24)."

My Mother's Prayer

One afternoon about the time that I got my promise for deliverance, Mother knelt before God for me. She asked God to deliver me as He had delivered Daniel from the lions' den and saved Shadrach, Meshach, and Abednego from the fiery furnace. Interceding in the language of God's Word, she prayed: "Can a woman forget her nursing child, and have no compassion on the son of her womb?" (Isa. 49:15). God answered her in the words of the prophet: "Whereas you have been forsaken and hated with no one passing through, I will make you an everlasting pride, a joy from generation to generation. . . . Then you will know that I, the Lord, am your Savior, and your Redeemer, the Mighty One of Jacob" (Isa. 60:15, 16*b*).

Mother was then led of the Holy Spirit to pray happily for more than two hours in the presence of God. Suddenly a very peaceful and strong voice came to her spirit, "Sung Ming is my beloved; I am looking after him and I will send him back."

Tears of thanks and joy flowed like water, washing her wounded spirit. She praised God for His greatness and goodness. God turned her weeping into gladness. She happily told my family that I was going to come back. Praise God! We Christians have the blessed experience of being guided and inspired by the same Holy Spirit.

The Prison Hospital

At that time in China, an army substation came to hold supreme power in every important community. Even the police were required to obey the orders of the army. Several weeks after my vision of heaven, I felt led by the Holy Spirit to write a request to the representatives of the army telling them of my condition. I asked the guard for a pencil and paper, which were supplied immediately. They thought I was finally willing to write my surrender and conversion to their way of thinking.

In January 1971 I was called out by three soldiers for an interview. Several times one of the three pushed my head with his two fingers, saying, "What did you think in these days? Will you change or still be stubborn?" I answered nothing but told them that I was seriously sick because of the long detention, and I asked for medical treatment. After physical examination by two doctors, and after checking the blood and urine tests in a prisoner's hospital, I was admitted to this hospital where I stayed 44 days.

I was put in a large ward with nearly 50 beds. How nice to have a bed again! I had not slept in one for more than two years. I was so weak and exhausted that when I got into bed I immediately fell sound asleep even though it was morning and the room was filled with medical officers and prisoners.

In the hospital I was given better food, with three meals each day. However, in the ward we could not talk to each other or move about freely. The door was always locked. Generally the treatment was better, but mentally it was nearly the same as in the prison. Every day we were required to read loudly *Mao's Quotations*.

This was my first experience in a hospital belonging to the prison system. We were required to attend indoctrination sessions called "The Struggling Meetings." As prisoner-patients we were forced to listen to indoctrination radio broadcasts. But even these contacts brought stimulation to my starved mind.

According to the theory of class struggle, every bad thought and deed was blamed on the bourgeois class. The Red Guards assigned the bad to the bourgeois, but every good thing was credited to the proletarian class. Red Guards, however, found it difficult to explain why the children and grandchildren raised in pure proletarian families went wrong. A former political writer for Mao Tse-tung was a pure descendant of a proletarian family. He had, however, ordered 2,955 persons killed among 84,000 political defendants in Hu Pei Province during the Cultural Revolution. That was only one case. These murderers were played up to be angels, and they made beautiful speeches. We prisoners were told that we should pay attention to them.

In the class struggle meetings, the teachers often dealt with men imprisoned for many years. Many of the prisoners had no interest in political propaganda. On the contrary, they wished to know about salvation in Jesus and the truths of God. I heard the head of the army personnel who resided in the prison say through a megaphone, "I wonder why these rotten troublemakers turn to searching for and believing God? Superstition! It is really unbelievable to me. Why? Why?"

He once asked a famous prisoner being sentenced for 21 years, a Catholic priest, to stand up and answer him. His answer was too soft for me to hear, but is was easy for me to understand. Everyone has a soul that is inclined to find its true Creator.

Dear Friend, if you are still an unbeliever, I sincerely encourage you to find the Truth, the real Creator—and find Him now. Why not seek Jesus and take Him as your Savior today? Do not wait until tomorrow. From my own experience I know that Christian faith is no superstition. A human being always seeks after God, even if he is in total despair. We sometimes yearn for Him also in our hours of great pleasure. God is real. He will be easily found if you seek Him. He takes care of everyone who knows Him.

An Attack by Satan

While in the prison hospital, I was first accused and then indicted by the devil. Satan is a spirit, but an evil spirit. He knows much more than anyone except God himself. Surely he is shrewder and more dangerous than any human being because of his long experience and power.

Usually my thoughts come from my own mind. As human beings we have the power to solve problems and to plan how to take the next steps—but the original impulse comes from the spirit world—either from God or from Satan. Our human brain has only derived powers. If the original thinking comes from God, communicated by the Holy Spirit, the result is beautiful and complete. The Bible tells us, "Every good thing bestowed and every perfect gift is from above, coming down from the Father of lights" (Jas. 1:17). However, if the original thinking is from Satan, the result will be bad and destructive.

In some decisions, we just do what we think or what we feel, but we should carefully examine every thought to determine if it comes from God or from the devil. From my experiences of failing God and also of successfully following Him I have learned that I do not have full control over my thinking. Even some scientific inventions have been given by God in moments of inspiration. I have read accounts of scientists testifying that their successful researches came from God. My own father gives God credit for an important personal discovery in his field of science.

Just as positive thoughts come from above, evil thoughts may originate with Satan. Early one morning in the prisoners' hospital, just as I woke up a cruel voice came to my spirit from the left and below. The voice said,

"You could be free and prosperous, and you could travel abroad; but only if you deny Jesus."

This voice nearly crushed my heart. My first fear was that the thought might be from my own mind. Insinuating that the idea was my own, the devil made me afraid by reminding me of a serious truth: "Whoever shall deny Me before men, I will also deny him before My Father who is in heaven" (Matt. 10:33).

But I knew that I had never entertained such a thought, even for a little while. Sometimes it was dangerous to confess Christ, but I had determined I would lay down my life rather than dishonor Him.

I thanked God that He gave me understanding to know that this evil idea was from Satan. I recalled the third temptation that Jesus met. The devil asked our Lord to fall down and worship him. In exchange the devil promised Jesus all the kingdoms of the world and the glory of them. I thought that I was being tempted with the same appeal, but I knew that I should follow my Lord even to death and to refuse the devil definitely. Then I prayed God to protect and save me because in my own strength I could not win a battle with Satan. I then sang a Chinese Christian song, "To God I must say yes, but to the devil I must say no." I trembled with terror for a long time, but gradually grew quieter. I felt that the demon had left me unwillingly, fearing the precious blood of Christ with His powerful name.

God gives us the freedom to choose His way or to go the way of evil. So He sometimes allows Christians to meet these struggles wishing to test us. If at that moment I had not recognized the voice, or if I had mistakenly followed its evil suggestion, I do not know what the result would have been. I might have gained success in the world, or I might have gone crazy. Thank God, I did not follow the evil voice, and I have been kept under His love and His care until now.

Satan the Deceiver

One Christian sister was punished beyond her endurance. She was forced to labor on a collective farm, and to be separated from her husband. One day the police lied to her. They told her that her husband had been put in prison and would be sentenced soon because of his Christian faith. They also threatened her, "If you are still stubborn, your future will be the same as your husband's."

She believed these words and lost all hope. That night she climbed a very high hill with sharp rocks below. Standing there she heard a voice in her heart from the left and below, "Why don't you finish your life tonight? What is the value for you to live in the world under such conditions? What is the hope for you to have a happy future? Maybe someday later you will also be put into prison. It is impossible to kill yourself there. Knowing the political situation, you had better finish yourself now. There is no hope, no future, no husband, no family—nothing at all to live for."

She did not realize that the voice came from the devil. She thought it was her own judgment—and it seemed completely right. She bit her finger and with her blood drew the cross on her blouse. She prayed for forgiveness—and jumped. But God took care of His own although there seemed no way she could avoid death. He caught her in His hands and saved her from death. There were serious skin and soft tissue injuries but no vital organs were damaged. She suffered bleeding and shock as a result of obeying the devil's words. But God loved her. He delivered her from death because she followed the devil's words unintentionally.

My wife experienced a similar temptation. One night as she was being chased by the Red Guards she went to a large well. The moon reflected bright and clear on the surface of the water. The night was quiet, and no one was with her. She was full of sadness and uncertainty. As she looked down into the well it seemed the moon was smiling at her.

Suddenly a voice in her inner mind said to her, "You are despised by your country. You are useless for the future. You dare not leave for another place because you are being followed. Why not drop into the still water now? Just once and then all trouble will be gone forever. Just once. Just once. Just once."

She was unconsciously bending forward over the edge of the well. Suddenly an unseen Power pulled her back. She was like one who had been awakened from a dream. God saved her and preserved her life for His further work.

Such experiences remind us of God's Word, "Do not give the devil an opportunity" (Eph. 4:27). Paul encourages us, "If we live by the Spirit, let us also walk by the Spirit" (Gal. 5:25). Therefore, let us be careful how we walk. Let us draw close to Christ.

My friend, if you are thinking that Jesus does not care for you, you can be sure that these thoughts come from the devil. He wants your soul to perish forever. I earnestly admonish you to put away such thoughts. Plead the blood of Jesus. Ask our Savior to deliver you from the attack of the devil. Christ alone can help, and He is ready to keep you by His power.

My Hospital Vision

One night God wonderfully revealed to me a vision in the hospital. I was in a big two-story church worshiping and praising God with all foreigners around me. I did not get any word from God before the vision disappeared, so I just wondered about it and asked myself, "Is this a common dream?" No. I knew clearly the difference between a vision and an ordinary dream. Therefore, I just kept it in my mind until I would know clearly the meaning. Today I can testify that it was shown to me to prepare me for worshiping and serving in the church in America. Thank God for His revealing Spirit and for His loving guidance.

After this vision I thought much about going out from my own land to fulfill God's will for me. But in the prison, how could I ever do it? Sometimes I believed in the certainty of my release, but sometimes I doubted and worried about the validity of these visions. I wished to see the proof of the visions that were not yet fulfilled.

Chapter 7

Released but Not Free

After 44 days in the hospital I was discharged with the diagnosis of liver cirrhosis and sent back to jail No. 9. It seemed there was no hope for me to be released.

The guards wanted me to write words of gratitude to the police because of the medical care. But how could I write such words sincerely? I did not feel it was a favor they had shown me. It was because of their cruelty that I had contracted the disease. So I did not write any word of thanks. Instead I reminded them that it was their guilt that had caused my illness. Once again they wished to soften my resistance and tried to get me to confess that it was my crime that had put me in prison. But I could not agree. Medical care was appreciated, but guilt was guilt. They used all kinds of tricky language seeking to bend right and wrong to their own standards. But right is right, and wrong is wrong. Jesus said the Christian is the light of the world and a saving salt in the earth. I felt that I could not follow their thinking and remain faithful to Christian standards of truth.

In this tension I could identify with Paul when he wrote: "For Thy sake we are being put to death all day long; we were considered as sheep to be slaughtered. But in all these things we overwhelmingly conquer through Him who loved us" (Rom. 8:36-37). I knew that God was with me, therefore I did not fear them any more.

The guards were amazed at my attitude and could only reply, "We will give you the final conclusion as soon as possible. You will get your deserved punishment according to your bad reaction to us." But I knew my destiny was in God's hands—not in theirs.

One morning in May 1971 a police officer about my own age came to the jail. Speaking to me in Mandarin, he said, "I will talk with you. Come out."

It was the first time in more than a year that anyone had talked to me about the charges against me. He led me into a special inquiry room and asked me to sit down opposite him. There were no handcuffs this time. Quietly and reasonably he told me, "You have been detained for nearly three years; the government is wanting to resolve your case quickly. In all of my experience, no one has kept their secrets without confessing them in prison. You have been here a long time and your case is nearly finished, but some points are still not clear. You are sick, and we should have concern for your body. Therefore your case should be settled quickly."

I thanked God for these words and told him confidently, "Justice will win."

On May 15, 1971, right after lunch, a guard called my number and said, "Quickly pack up all your things and bring them out."

Instantly a flood of murmurs broke the silence and depression of prison room No. 9. "Old Lagger is going to be set free! Congratulations!"

Others murmured, "No, it is impossible for him to be free. Only three days ago the head of the guards shouted loudly in front of the door, 'You will get your deserved punishment because of your bad reaction to us.' He is going to be sentenced."

Still others said, "His case ought to be resolved. It is more bearable to be sentenced unjustly than to stay here such a long time. Only Old Lagger could bear sitting on the floor for three years."

I waved my hand to the prisoners, and many of them bid me a friendly good-bye. When I got to the front yard of the prison, the policeman who had talked to me earlier came toward me smiling, and said, "Today I am going to send you home. You may have medical treatment there, but your every act still must be reported to us daily. Your case is not finished. You are still a prisoner, but a prisoner at home because of your disease."

The head of the guards and some others stood scowling and unhappy. They did not want to see me released. The policeman asked me, "Did you know that your wife has been captured and imprisoned?"

I answered, "No. I have not been told."

He said, "Her attitude was much better than yours. She has been back staying with her mother for more than a year."

My heart nearly burst with joy. I recollected the vision that God had showed me that we would meet together in the Village of Faith and Righteousness. It seemed that God's vision was to be fully accomplished. But the policeman cautioned me, "You cannot inform your wife that you have been sent home. You cannot contact her. You cannot do anything without letting us know. If you do, you will bear the full responsibility. We will continue to investigate your case. Now endorse your name on the back of your release papers."

Having signed the papers, I was led out of the jail. My father and a brother had been informed, and they were waiting outside to take me home. Because I was still a prisoner we knew that we dared not show our emotions when we met. If we did, these guards would accuse us of another political crime. We all restrained our tears.

As we left the jail some of the guards were watching us closely. Because I was walking slowly a guard came up behind me and kicked my left leg, shouting, "Why do you walk so slowly? Be quick."

I was nearly knocked down, but I understood he was testing me to see if I really was very sick. He was still not willing for me to be released.

When we got to the home of my parents, we hugged each other. But since we could trust no one, not even our neighbors, our tears of joy were shed silently and secretly. I was astonished at the way God had led me, and my heart was full of praises. We knelt down and thanked God for His protection and His deliverance. Quietly we sang Psalm 23 together: "Yea, though I walk through the valley of the shadow of death, I will fear no evil, for thou art with me, thy rod and thy staff they comfort me."

My parents insisted that I go to bed immediately and remain there because my whole body was swollen. But in spite of my illness, I could only praise God. With the Psalmist, my spirit sang: "I will give Thee thanks with all my heart; I will sing praises to Thee . . . I will bow down toward Thy holy temple, and give thanks to Thy name for Thy lovingkindness and Thy truth . . . Though I walk in the midst of trouble, Thou wilt revive me; Thou wilt stretch forth Thy hand against the wrath of my enemies, and Thy right hand will save me. The Lord will accomplish what concerns me; Thy lovingkindness, O Lord, is everlasting; do not forsake the work of Thy hands" (Ps. 138:1-2, 7-8).

How thankful and excited I was after 33 months of captivity to be back home. It was unbelievable. All things seemed new. It was as though I had been raised to life from the grave. Now I understood why Jesus did not go to cure Lazarus immediately even though He knew that Lazarus was mortally ill. From my experience I can see that He was waiting for the right time to show the greater glory of God to everyone. Even Mary and Martha did not fully believe that Jesus was able to raise a dead brother from his grave.

Jesus' greater miracle showed His love and power to all the people staying with Mary and Martha. Then the glory of His name was spread abroad.

O God, if You had taken all my troubles away at the time I was crying to You, I would not have recognized You so deeply, and I would not have understood my fellowmen when they are weak and heavily burdened. O Lord, if I had had peace and comfort all of my life, I would not have sympathy for others when they are in trouble.

Our Chinese philosopher Confucius said, "The determined scholar and the man of virtue will not seek to live at the expense of injuring their virtue. They will sacrifice their lives to preserve their virtue complete." And again, "If a man can for one day subdue himself and return to propriety, all under heaven will ascribe perfect virtue to him." Sometimes if a man sacrifices himself for the truth, even to death, it is really worthwhile in the sight of God.

Released but Under Attack

Soon after I came back, some neighbors still wished us to fall into the political pit once again. They rushed into my room, shouting, "You are under house arrest. You are still a prisoner. Is this not true? Be honest or we will put you into prison again. You are under the supervision of the local street government office. You cannot go out freely. You cannot speak freely as we do. You cannot engage in your professional work; all you can do is cooking, washing, learning Mao's work, and confessing and writing down your crimes. Bad and stubborn you are!"

My heart was sad when I heard these words. I wondered why these people were so hostile. Why would they show no mercy even though I had done them no harm? I felt akin to the lament of the Psalmist, "Because of all my adversaries, I have become a reproach, especially to my neighbors, and an object of dread to my acquaintances;

those who see me in the street flee from me. I am forgotten as a dead man, out of mind, I am like a broken vessel. For I have heard the slander of many, terror is on every side; while they took counsel together against me, they schemed to take away my life" (Ps. 31:11-13).

But God used this experience to teach me faith and trust. The more bitter the taste I got from men, the sweeter the taste of the Word of God that He gave me.

First Days at Home

The fourth day after my return, a knock sounded at the front gate in the late afternoon. It was not as loud as when the Red Guards came; it must be some relative or some Christian friend come to visit us. When the door was opened, my wife was standing outside. She said, "Do not be afraid. I come here with the permission of my local street political leader to visit you."

My family replied with terror, "Sung Ming has been released for only three days. He was warned by the police that he could not contact you and that he could not meet you. If he even visited with you, he would be put into prison again for disobeying their command. Your coming shows that he has violated the law. Who told you that he had come home?"

Min Tsu only smiled and said, "Why are you so afraid? I have permission to come here to visit all of you. God showed me a vision and urged me to come to your house."

Then my wife was led into the room where we were sitting. We were stunned when we saw her. No one could say a word, but our tears flowed as she began to tell us about her vision that she had seen four days before.

She said, "I was alone in a small boat. The wind was blowing hard and the waves beat against me. I could not see the shore and began to worry about how I would get to land. Just at that moment I saw a man at the other end of the boat. He picked up the oars and pulled on them three times. Like an arrow the boat shot quickly across the water and touched the shore. I jumped out on the sand and saw a beautiful church in front of me—a building that I had never seen before. The sound of the church bell and the organ attracted me. I started eagerly toward the door. Suddenly I remembered that I had left something in the boat. As I turned to see if the boat was still there, I awakened."

Min Tsu's experience was not a dream. It was a vision, different from ordinary dreams. As she puzzled about what it meant, a voice in her spirit said, "Go quickly to Sung Ming's parents' home to visit them."

She had never entertained such a thought before because of the serious political situation. She had been warned many times by the police not to visit my family, or she would be arrested again. At first she thought it better to be cautious and to stay at home. But her spirit was really troubled until she began to obey the voice of the Holy Spirit. She prayed, "O God, if this is Your command, let me be successful when I ask my political leader in the Street Office."

She had then gone to the officer at once and asked if she could visit her husband's parents. The officer readily agreed, saying, "You may if you wish."

Without delay my wife took a pedicab to our house. The three strokes of the oars were just equal to the three days that I had been at home.

We came to understand why the police had warned me not to inform or to meet my wife. They wished to create conflict between our families and between us. They still hoped that one family would not influence the other against the government. If God had not shown Min Tsu the vision telling her to come to see us, probably someone would have told her family that I had come home and did not want her to know. A deep misunderstanding could have developed. When they had warned me not to see her, I thought I understood their evil motive, but I was helpless to resolve the dilemma. So were my parents and my brothers. All of us were blocked by the political pressure. But the Almighty God, the omniscient and omnipotent One, full of mercy and kind care, showed His love and favor to us. Thanks be to God!

We both felt that it was not right to separate wife and husband. My wife went back to her mother's home to pray about it. I remained at my parents' home for what medical care I could get. The police did nothing to care for me. At this time my parents and I received only 15 yen per month each. There was no money to see a doctor; no money to go to a hospital for tests; no money to buy nutritious food or medicine. The police released me from prison to die because the prisoner-hospital had told them that I could not live longer than two years. The cirrhosis of my liver was an irreversible disease.

I was very sick. My liver was enlarged and my whole body swollen. The psychological environment was also bad for me. My family told me many disturbing things that upset me. I was told that many men were still being shot for opposing the government. Before these men were put to death the police bound them from neck to feet so that they could not even shout or move. To warn the people, they then put the victims on a truck and drove slowly through the streets to the place of execution. These public displays told the people that if they dared rebel against the Gang of Four, the same sentence would fall upon them. My family said to me, "Every day we worry about you because of the unlawful times. It is especially dangerous before the date set for the public trial."

Returning Health, and Home

Some days I felt more troubled than in the prison because there they did not let me know anything. Disease, poverty, terror, and uncertainty made me once again lack courage. I did not have the faith to go forward. I knew that I was sinking into deep despair, but I was so weak that I could not fight it. I was like an exhausted traveler under the burning desert sun.

One night about two weeks after I returned home, I heard a spiritual voice very profound and clear, speaking in English,

"Hold fast of Him and you will see the deeds of God."

The voice lifted me instantly from that deep pit of despair. I thanked God for His unceasing tender love to me even in those terrible hours when doubts had assailed me. I really could not understand why the King of heaven and earth took thought of me. I was not worthy of His care. Men forsook me but God received me. In my weakness I was strengthened again and again by His unspeakably great love.

I ignored the words of the prison hospital doctors who had said that I could not live two years longer. The words were a true medical prognosis, and I knew the seriousness of my disease. But I did not worry about it. I had peace of mind because I knew that God would not forsake those who sought Him. I understood and resisted my human weaknesses, and I prayed earnestly that I might trust Him fully. Day after day I gradually recovered and became stronger. I did not take medicine except for vitamins. Even the police who came each month as part of their surveillance marveled that I was getting better. After one year I was in completely good health.

After three months my wife got permission from her local leader to move to my home. In our home every morning we knelt privately for at least one hour in the presence of God in prayer. From the devil there came terrors and worrying. But through prayer they were all driven away.

"Hold fast of Him and you will see the deeds of God." This word lighted me through dark times and even today still gives me strength. I believe that it is a sure word from God for everyone who is under trials.

Chapter 8

Min Tsu—My Wife's Story

I also was born into a Christian family. As a child I went to church with my mother and older sisters and brother. I learned to pray and to sing hymns in the church. It was a beautiful and reverent atmosphere. In childhood, as a good girl, I understood only that I should be honest, faithful, hardlearning and hardworking, good to everyone, sympathetic with the poor and needy, and showing love to all.

After I graduated from the conservatory in Peking, I performed as a concert pianist and began to know more about what life was like outside of Christian circles. I realized very clearly the difference between Christians and non-Christians. I saw many kinds of evil in the world and recognized that true goodness is totally contrary to evil. I saw more and more the two faces of human nature. There was a smiling face, but also there was the dark reflection of an evil heart.

The period of the Gang of Four was a time of triumph for evil human minds. The spirit of the devil could be seen, and the hearts of the righteous were deeply grieved. No one could avoid the disasters that resulted—not even the Gang of Four and their colleagues could escape from these tragedies. All have been sentenced for their crimes by the national supreme court.

As told in my husband's story, following his arrest, the authorities required that I send his mother back to her hometown on September 19, 1968. Right after she left I was admitted to the hospital for treatment because of extreme cruelty toward us. My health was seriously damaged; my heart beat very rapidly and breathing became almost impossible. When I went to the hospital, I was alone, and there was no one to sign admission papers for me. No one knew me, and I had only a little money in my pocket—not enough to pay the bill. I stayed in the hospital for two days, then had to leave for lack of money.

Desolation

I went to a Christian sister's home. She comforted me and we prayed together. I wore all black clothing instead of my favorite colors. I looked like a widow—I felt like a widow—no smiling, no happiness, and no joy. The loss of my husband made me discouraged in spirit, and my body grew weaker. Some Christians and other friends wished to help me forget my sorrows, but how could I? The more they tried, the more bitter I felt. No one could console me. Nothing could satisfy me anymore. Like Job, I began to wish I had never been born. I could hardly praise God because my husband had been taken away only five days after our marriage. Depressed and full of inward pain, I longed for someone who could give me real help.

One day I went to seek help from an older Christian sister. She had fasted one meal each day and prayed for the Chinese church every day for more than 10 years. When I saw her I burst into tears. She prayed earnestly with me and sang a Bible verse set to a Chinese tune: "Give me your heart, my son, and let your eyes delight in my ways" (Prov. 23:26).

It was remarkable how this precious verse strengthened my weak spirit and made me glad. She showed me other Bible truths: "Every man's way is right in his own eyes, but the Lord weighs the hearts. To do righteousness and justice is desired by the Lord more than sacrifice"

(Prov. 21:2-3). "Do not fret because of evildoers, or be envious of the wicked; for there will be no future for the evil man; the lamp of the wicked will be put out" (Prov. 24:19-20).

With her spiritual help I went home strengthened, but I asked myself many questions. They tumbled in rapid succession from my troubled mind. I could find no satisfying answers to any of them.

Could it be worse? Is my life as bitter as it can be? Is there any hope it will get better? Ever? Is there any possibility that my husband will come back, even though I was told he would be sentenced for at least 15 years?

What serious crime has he committed? Why did he never tell me before we decided to get married? Is he really a criminal?

Where are my mother and my family members? Where are my parents-in-law? Where is my husband, and what is he doing?

Hunted by the Police

One day I was invited to a park by some friends to cheer me up. They rented a boat and were rowing and singing. Their intentions were good but my heavy heart was not lifted. If it had fallen from the boat, it surely would have sunk to the bottom of the lake like a stone.

I had begun teaching some piano students in order to earn a little money for living. That afternoon I was scheduled to go to a student's home to give him a lesson, so the boat ride was interrupted. The boat stopped at the dock, and I joined the others getting off. Suddenly I felt someone pulling me off balance. I stumbled and fell with my right arm in the water. The sleeve of my dress was soaked so that I could not go on to my student's home. I returned to the friend's house where I was living. While changing my dress I learned that some policemen with more than 20 Red

Guards were hiding around the student's home waiting for me. Someone had betrayed my schedule to them. But it was not the time for me to be arrested; God helped me to escape their trap. From that day I was a hunted woman.

Running for My Life

Several weeks later another Christian friend came secretly after dark to see me. She told me that nearly all of my acquaintances and friends had been approached by the police to learn my present address. Some were being held in detention because they would not speak. She advised me, "So far as I know none of these friends has betrayed you, but you should leave this city as quickly as possible."

I said, "Where shall I go without a place to stay?"

She replied, "I have some friends in a small city not far from here. I will introduce you to them to stay in their house. But the first problem is to get you out of this city. We cannot help you because too many people know us, but I will try to work it out for you."

She left, but came back in about two hours telling me that my picture as a wanted criminal was posted in nearly all the stations, docks, and airports. I was stunned. I had become a criminal almost overnight. How could I deal with the disgrace and fear? I burst into uncontrollable tears. When I grew calmer, my friend recommended a young man about 25 years of age to help me.

"He is a truck driver for a factory. He can drive you out of the city to my friend's home. He is a friend of mine; a good man, but he is not yet a Christian. Go with him now without hesitation. He is waiting outside."

Before we left, the young man said to me, "Tell me the whole story. Let me understand you completely. If you are not a real criminal I would like to help you even if I am put in prison for doing it."

I told him everything, and he realized my innocence. He said, "Follow me. I must help you if I possibly can." I thanked God for sending him my way. The next morning we would try to leave the city in his truck, though it would be dangerous for him and for me. He hid me with cargo in the trailer and drove alone in the cab. We had to pass through the city wall; that would be the most crucial moment. As we approached the gate, he saw many officers on duty. They were carefully inspecting all vehicles. Even the pedestrians were stopped and checked. How could we ever pass? When they came to our truck they simply asked for his identification, and wonder of wonders, did not open the trailer. God was with us. Sometime later we reached our destination. My new friend had proved to be entirely honest and trustworthy.

I was in a city that I did not know and I had no certificate of permission to be there. I was received in the house of friends whom I had not met before, even though it was extremely dangerous for them. If the Red Guards came some night to search the house, I would be found and handed over to the police.

The plan was for me to pretend to be a visitor in the city for several weeks. Every morning I had to leave the house where I stayed, pretending to make a tour around the town. Some days I borrowed a bike, riding through street after street without any destination. I stopped when I felt tired. When I was standing on a street corner to rest I feared somebody would know me or doubt my story. Occasionally I rode to the farms or to a suburb of the city alone in order to avoid the attention of others. I had no water, so when I grew thirsty I had to drink from the creeks. There was no place to rest when I felt exhausted except to sit on a stone or on the ground. I had no food except one or two pieces of candy that I carried in my pocket; no company but the birds and a few wild rabbits. I wondered why I still lived in this world.

But God did not forsake me. One day when I was riding the bike, Psalm 23 came to my mind: "Yea, though I walk through the valley of the shadow of death, I will fear no evil ... Thou preparest a table before me in the presence of mine enemies: thou anointest my head with oil; my cup runneth over" (KJV). Again and again the words flowed through my mind.

I rode out to the farm and sat down on the ground to argue with God. "O my Lord, I am being chastened fiercely, and I suffer more than any girl can bear. Am I stronger than other women? Why do You give me these verses? Is it really possible for me to have a table spread in the presence of my enemies?"

Then I grew calmer and reflected, "It is good enough if I am not captured, and it will be wonderful if my husband can be released." I could find no other meaning, but these verses brought me much peace. I could hardly understand myself, because I forgot that I was being hunted. I began to sing some hymns and to repeat Psalm 23 aloud. I was happy that day in my communion with God.

Friends Indeed

Five of my friends, including the young man who helped me move, took turns on weekends coming down to see me and to take care of me. They moved me from one city to another and from one farm home to another. They supplied me with what money I needed to stay alive. At the time I could not give them anything, but I prayed for them and began to introduce these friends to Jesus. I tried to explain to them why Christians suffer in the world so much more than unbelievers. I said, "If I had not had these troubles I would not have met you and could not have told you the story of our Lord and Savior. God has let it be hard for me physically but it is good for you spiritually. I praise God for all of you."

I soon learned that the young man who had first helped me was a heavy smoker and drinker. He felt there was no justice and no righteousness at all in the world. He was understandably troubled because there seemed no way he could get rid of his frustrations except to drink large amounts of strong wine.

Having heard the message of salvation from me, he stopped drinking and began to read the Bible and to pray every day. His broken heart was comforted because he had found the fountain of Living Water. He accepted Jesus as his Savior, and the other four were greatly influenced by him. God really blessed him for his faith. Eventually he was miraculously brought out from China and came to America where he built a good life for his family.

We met him again when we came to America. At that time he told me how he had lost his job as punishment for helping me. He had gone to the blood bank every month and sold 100 cc's of blood for 20 yen for his living. When I learned that, I prayed again that God would reward him both in body and in spirit. I knew that "God is not one to show partiality, but in every nation the man who fears Him and does what is right, is welcome to Him" (Acts 10:34-35).

"In Dens and Caves of the Earth"

During those first days of my flight I stayed in any one home only a week or 10 days because my friends could not tell their friends the real plight that I was in. On the farms I was bitten by mosquitoes, fleas, and other insects. In the poorest farmer's home there was no place for me to sleep except beside the pig pen. The odor and the snoring of the pigs was something I had never experienced before. In the daytime I usually moved about aimlessly. If it rained or thundered, I sat under a tree alone or crawled into a hole or cave. Sometimes at night I had no place to sleep except in a ditch or a grove. Wind, rain, snow, and silence were my cruel and constant companions.

I always carried a small Bible with me, and often read Heb. 11:36-38: "And others experienced mockings and scourgings, yes, also chains and imprisonment. They were stoned, they were sawn in two, they were tempted, they were put to death with the sword; they went about in sheepskins, in goatskins; being destitute, afflicted, ill-treated (men of whom the world was not worthy), wandering in deserts and mountains and caves and holes in the ground."

I could only cry to God asking for all of us His mercy and deliverance from our present hard circumstances. If I had not been a Christian I would have killed myself. When my spirit was the lowest I usually asked God, "How many girls in the world can bear such afflictions? You know I am weak both in my body and in my spirit. Why do You allow all these things to happen to me? Death would be better than these pains. Why have You set me as an animal in the wilderness without a home or a room to live in?"

When I murmured, the Holy Spirit often reminded me of the words of Jesus, "The foxes have holes, and the birds of the air have nests; but the Son of Man has nowhere to lay His head" (Matt. 8:20). He taught me that a Christian should learn how to suffer in the world as well as to enjoy the companionship of Jesus. We are His disciples, and we cannot be higher than our Lord. After these experiences I knew how deeply Jesus loved me. He had sacrificed His life without complaint. Remembering Him, I repented for feeling sorry for myself. I resolved to be a faithful Christian publicly and privately. But I knew it would not be easy.

Twice I seriously contemplated suicide, but God saved me from death. One account has already been told by my husband—I felt a strong urge to throw myself into a well, but God spared me. The second occurred one night when I was on a large passenger boat taking me from a city to yet another farm. I could not get to sleep. Some power not of my own will seemed to pull me out of my room to the deck of the boat. No one was with me. I stood at the rail and watched the water running swiftly around the boat.

Suddenly the thought entered my mind, Why continue to worry about your future? Why tolerate all of this depression? You need only to jump into the water to end this meaningless existence. All your trouble will be gone. This way is the easiest and the quickest. Why not do it now?

I knew that it was from the devil, but I could not get away from the impulse. The course seemed right under the circumstances—but I hesitated a few moments. My girl friend awakened and saw that I was not in bed. She jumped up and ran out on the deck. When she saw me bent over and looking down into the water she shouted, "Min Tsu, what are you doing? Come back to your bed."

It seemed as if I had awakened from a bad dream. I trembled as I followed her back to our room. If she had come five minutes later, I would already have flung myself into the river. But God had arranged for her to call my name just in time to save me. Deliverance came from God.

From that day on I began to be strengthened by God's Word. I asked Him to deliver me and to be my Help always. The whole situation outside was getting worse, but my spirit was getting stronger and stronger.

Sometimes I slipped into the city where I had lived, to try to find a place to sleep. One night the weather was so cold that I dared not stay out in the woods or in a hole. I disguised myself with dark glasses and went into the city to ask a good sister to help me for the night. She invited me in, although she was afraid to do it. I asked her, "Are you worried for taking me in as a guest?"

She answered kindly, "I never refuse anyone who comes to me in need. You have come here in need, and God knows it, so He will protect us. Come in. Have some food and get a good sleep tonight."

After I had eaten the best meal I had had in weeks, I quickly dropped off to sleep. But about nine o'clock in the evening, there was a big noise outside. Someone shouted, "If there is anyone in this area who does not have a citizen's certificate, he must come out and let us know. We are going to search every family and check every home."

It was the Red Guards. Unfortunately, I was in my friend's home without a certificate. If they found me, both she and I would be arrested. Instead of sleeping, we prayed for God to send His angels to surround our room and keep us safe. He responded to our earnest prayer. No one came to our room though there were many Red Guards searching every home. After they went away, we quietly praised God for His protection.

I was so tired that I went back to bed and fell asleep quickly. But this good Christian sister knelt beside my bed and prayed for me through the whole night. I often felt her love pat, and the touch of her hand on my back and hair. In Christ's name she had compassion for me. I was deeply comforted by the sound sleep and by her tender love. I shall never forget that night in her home, because once again I had experienced that God was with me. He had not left me alone. He cared for me.

The next morning God's good sister sent me on my way with some food and some homemade candies. I did not know where to go, so wandered back into the country where I had lived in the wild. I was a girl of 25, pursued as a political criminal although I had never had a gun, had never hurt anyone, and had made no opposition to my government. I could not understand why I had been declared a criminal and why they had put such a crime on me. The Chinese have a proverb: "The king intends his minister to die; the minister cannot but die. The military father intends to kill his son; the son cannot escape." I was a little person, and the authorities intended for me to die. The political crime claimed by them was put on me without proof.

I now lived as an animal. I feared the wilderness and the animals, but I feared those human animals more. How long could I live?

Arrested

Four of the friends who had been helping me were under arrest and in separate cells. They were accused of helping an enemy of the government. Only the young truck driver was now free to help me. We had agreed to meet each other one morning at eleven o'clock at the bus stop. I waited for him until one o'clock in the afternoon, but he did not come. I was sure something had happened to him, because he had never been late before when meeting me. He knew it was dangerous for me to stand in public for a long time. Just before I decided to leave I saw him in a bus with a frown on his face. He motioned me to go farther away, then got off at the next stop and walked back to meet me. He quickly told me in a low voice that the police had questioned him about his contacts with me and about the antigovernment activities they claimed that we had been engaged in.

"I was ordered to write information about you and all the others involved. My political leader ordered me to remain in the factory. I was not to leave without permission. But I slipped out to let you know that now I am also facing terrible danger. Probably this is the last time we can meet. I will be punished if I return to work. I will not betray you even if I am put into prison. So good-bye for now."

I saw him go for the last time and was worried about him. I was sure that I would be arrested soon because I could not continue my flight without the help he had been giving me.

On April 26, 1970, I was recognized by some spies when I came to a friend's house for help. They went to the police and told them that I was in that house. The police waited outside my friend's home and caught me when I stepped out. I was taken to the police station and confronted by policemen, Red Guards, and those who had betrayed me. The police from my native city were also there. I was faced by the same man who had arrested my husband and had stolen our money for his personal use. The important officer of the present government smiled at me disdainfully, saying, "Where will you go now? You are in our hands. Though you had wings you could not fly from our snare. No tricky counterrevolutionist can escape from the hand of the Chinese people."

I just looked at him and said nothing. A woman bailiff searched my pockets and my whole body. I was told to sign my name on the back of my detention paper, then two bailiffs took me to the jail. I shed no tears because the well of my sorrow was nearly dried up from all I had suffered during the year and a half since my husband's arrest. I had lived a hard life in the desert, in ditches, in fields, and in underground concrete bomb shelters. Imprisonment was just another kind of bitterness to me. Anyway, I knew that whether I lived or died, I belonged to Christ. I prayed a simple prayer in the words of the Scripture: "I entreated Thy favor with all my heart; be gracious to me according to Thy word" (Ps. 119:58).

The police questioned me several times before I was returned to my husband's town. A woman and a young policeman took me back by train. Fortunately my hands were not cuffed, but the woman was cruel to me. When I closed my eyes because of fatigue, she pounded the table and shouted, "You reactionary element, we will kill you after you have arrived. You are prohibited to sleep. Stay awake and consider what you should do next, resist continually or surrender completely."

I made no answer because I had already entrusted my life to God. I had decided to keep my soul pure without stain or sin. Wonderfully, Jesus gave me peace—true peace—in my heart. I did not fear what they threatened, and I did not resent what they said to me. I trusted that Christ would carry me safely through no matter what evils came. A line of a precious song gave me courage:

> On Christ, the solid Rock, I stand;
> All other ground is sinking sand.

I did not know what the next hour would bring to me, but I looked to Jesus and learned to lean hard on His powerful arm.

Put in Prison

I was jailed in the same prison, room No. 13, as my husband, but neither of us knew that the other was there. There were 12 other women in my room. All were guilty of crimes except two of us who were political prisoners. The room was small; about 7 by 10 feet. Each of us thus had a space on the floor about 6 feet long and 2 feet wide. There was no rest room; only a urine tub. Each woman was allowed one gallon of water per day for all purposes. In the room there were no chairs, no table, and no beds. We were treated like animals. Really, the cows in the government-controlled commune and the horses in the military stables were treated better than the prisoners.

Our two meals a day were of very poor quality. I had seen pigs on the farms that fared better. Because of the foul food, I had no appetite. My cell mates wondered why

I did not feel hungry, and they wished to eat a part of my food but it was prohibited. They said to me, "You are crazy. Do you wish to die?"

The guard warned me, "If you refuse to eat, we have the responsibility to force you. We will open your mouth and insert a long feeding tube down your throat, or give you injections of glucose intravenously."

I was so upset that I replied, "This food is worse than you feed a pig. How can a human being eat it? If you expect us to eat it, will you please eat some of it first?"

The other prisoners thought the guard would punish me, but he did not. Instead he opened the door and took me to his office. There he said to me, "This is a jail; we cannot treat you as the hospital treats a patient. But because of your health we will allow you glucose powder."

Every day they sent me vitamins and glucose powder. I ate these instead of the filthy solid food. The guard told me they had not treated any other prisoner this way. I was amazed that they had been so lenient with me, but I think now I know the reason. The police and the guards both used the soft approach toward me, hoping that I would be persuaded to cooperate with them. I did not, however, give them any of the statements they had hoped to get.

In the Prison Hospital

Due to lack of nutrition and to some emotional stress, my heart rate jumped up above 200 beats per minute. I was sent to the prison hospital six times for examination and finally was admitted as a patient. It was a large hospital completely inside the prison walls. Here I saw for the first time the so-called humane treatment of prisoners. Many of these inmates had been here for at least 5 years; some had been sentenced to more than 20. Most of those who had been sentenced to more than 10 years were political prisoners, including Protestant Christians and Catholics. I asked myself why these good people should have to suffer for so many years. They were not robbers or thieves; nor were they damaging public morals. They had committed no crimes against the law.

Near my bed were two good sisters, from a Christian organization called "Little Flock." They had been sentenced to more than 20 years in prison. Their chest bones and spines were now deformed and protruding in front and back as a result of the long period of detention and punishments. They groaned from the pain, but no one was allowed to visit them. Some of the nurses mocked them, "Why does your God not come to cure your diseases? You are evil doers, so be quiet."

I recognized them because I had heard them preaching when I was a little girl. My heart ached for them but we were forbidden to talk to each other. I could only pray for them, asking God to release them quickly. I had been told that they had already served out their sentences. I wondered if God had allowed me to be imprisoned at this time so that I could testify that they were faithful unto death. After my release, I was told that both died in the prison under suspicious circumstances soon after the completion of their sentences. I am glad that God allowed me to see them face-to-face, so that I can be a true and faithful witness to record the final stories of these two Christian martyrs in the history of the Chinese church.

I stayed in the hospital for 13 days, but my accelerated heartbeat continued without improvement. When they discharged me from the hospital and sent me back to jail, I could neither walk nor talk when they questioned me. I was a very weak Christian, but I wanted to follow the good way of the saints who had gone before. I had determined to sacrifice my life if necessary to be faithful to Christ. God was true to His promise: He "will not allow you to be tempted beyond what you are able, but with the temptation will provide the way of escape also, that you may be able to endure it" (1 Cor. 10:13).

Released

Unexpectedly on August 1, 1970, a young police officer (the same one who stole 500 yen from my husband's file) told me to get my belongings ready to leave. I did not know where I was going, but thought I would be sentenced and then transferred to a different prison. I was so sick that I could not move, so several prisoners helped me pack my few possessions. Then I said: "I am ready."

The guard opened the door and the policeman helped me out to the front yard. There he said to me, "We are releasing you to go home today because of your sickness. It is our policy to be humane to every prisoner. Nevertheless, your case is far from finished. We hope you will believe the government and because of our fair treatment you will change your mind and help us win over your bourgeois family. Your husband stubbornly resists us. He has now been imprisoned for two years but he has not yet changed his reactionary stand. We wish you to write down all that he has talked to you about and tell us what he has done so that we may help him change his mind. Your oldest brother and your mother are waiting to pick you up."

I was very sick and my head was not clear, so I did not answer him. I was too weak to reply. A little later, I reflected on my experience and my recent release. I had seen many prisoners who were more seriously ill than I. They were still held. Why had I been released? Why this more humane treatment for me? Was it a trick? I finally decided either they could not find a reason to detain me or they thought I was so near death that there was no point in keeping me.

The guard opened the gate and my brother came to hug me and take me out.

Under House Arrest

I stayed at home under surveillance. The police and the Red Guards worked together, coming to my home often to ask questions. Among the police who came was the dishonest officer who had stolen my husband's money in order to pay for his own wedding. Sometimes the police and guards were courteous. On other days they were angry and ill-tempered. No matter what their attitude, I tried to avoid trouble by remaining poised and courteous. I knew that my husband and I were innocent. God must be allowing these things to happen to us in order to purify us and to test our faith and our love for Him. I had abandoned myself to God's will, and I believed that He would take care of us.

Reunited with My Husband

From my experiences I can testify that God is alive and God is love. If we believe in Him and trust Him He will care for us. Praise the Lord. Faith in God is not a superstition. God is faithful to His children, and they shine as lights in the dark world. We Chinese have a proverb, "Temporary winning or failing is due to our strength or weakness; Permanent victory is due to the truth." Jesus is that Truth. By His powerful hand and sweet love, I was finally reunited with my husband.

After six months I determined to break the police order that forbade us living together. I asked the political head in our block, "What law in the Chinese Constitution forbids husband and wife from living together?"

She was dazed by the appeal to truth, and answered, "There is no such law."

Then I asked, "Since there is no law against it, may I move to my husband's home? He is sick and I can help him."

The officer was silent for a moment, then she said, "Since you are determined to go, you have my permission."

That evening I went to my husband's home and I remained with him. I had no work except caring for him and for our one small room. We prayed together every morning asking God for His continued protection because there were still many people being sentenced publicly and put into prison. We asked God to show His power once again and for His name's sake to move the police to release us. We were both greatly helped by the promise God had given to my husband: "Hold fast of Him and you will see the deeds of God." These words encouraged us when we were afraid and strengthened us when we were weak.

Both of us were usually self-reliant. We disliked being dependent. After I grew stronger, I especially felt ashamed to be supported by others. We wished to live alone, and we wished to work so that we could support ourselves. This desire is normally right and good, but sometimes God permits circumstances that make us depend on others and depend on Him. He requires us to surrender all our mind, will, and strength to Him so that we can learn to trust and obey Him. This seemed to be the lesson that we needed to learn. It might seem easy to learn such a lesson in the home of one's family, but it was hard for us.

I was able to help my husband with his recovery from cirrhosis of the liver, and we thanked God for every bit of His help and blessing.

Released but Under Suspicion

On May 14, 1972, a policeman came to our home, ordering us to go to the police station for the final decision of our cases. We reported there at eight o'clock the next morning. The police declared us free from their point of view without any further punishment: "From today your cases are finished. We have researched all the doubtful points of your families, and we have not found any crime against the law. You are both now free from house arrest." They continued with their usual lies, "You may live wherever you wish, and you may travel wherever you like. You may do and speak whatever you want." Then they warned us, "You may not leave the way of our proletarian society and the thinking of Mao. If you leave it, you will be guilty of a crime, and you will be put into prison once again.

"Remember that both of you come from the bourgeois class. Because of this, your thinking is far from that of the proletariat. If you do not change to the proletarian stand, you will probably return to captivity. Your minds are nonproletarian, and you have committed serious political mistakes, such as seeking more knowledge and living for yourselves rather than for the Chinese people.

"You also admire the new achievements of Western countries, wishing to learn from America and Japan, and you plan to leave your motherland. These are superstitions of your whole family. We do not care about your parents' superstition because they are old and will have little effect on our society. But you are young. We cannot allow you to spread those superstitions and influence our newborn socialistic generations.

"The final decision for both of you is: We can find no evidence of crime against either of you, but the husband has committed a very serious political mistake in his mind, and the wife follows him. It was right for us to put both of you in custody. Do you agree with our decision? If so, sign both of your names on this paper of declaration."

Because of the political pressure, we had no choice. We signed our names and accepted our release. They were always right, and we were always wrong. That was the logic of those dark times.

We did wish to learn more of the sciences and arts in order to serve our society that much better. Great inventions were coming from the learning and research of other countries. We admired their efforts and wanted to learn from them. We could not follow these desires without getting into deeper trouble. If one sought learning, the Red Guards immediately gave you a "cap"—a political label: rightist, pro-Western, traitor, reactionary, a man with a serious political blunder.

Because leaders of the Cultural Revolution feared educated people, they sent them to do manual labor on the farms. Their slogans were: "Labor is the greatest blessing in the world." "Labor will purify everyone who has fallen into the muddy ditch of the bourgeois class." "Labor can reform one's mind to think like the working class, the peasant, and the soldier."

Another political term was "Grasping your queue." It meant that the authorities were watching everyone's acts and words, grasping at anything that seemed suspicious. These political devices and oppressive measures made the people in the whole nation frightened and miserable. In their opposition to belief in Jesus, those leaders were really ignorant of God's works and of His love. They had no reason to say any word against Christian faith except that Christ calls for truth and righteousness. Also Christ calls for our supreme loyalty. We believed in Jesus not only because we had learned about Him from the Bible but also because we had personally experienced His reality. We could not deny what we knew.

We were aware that the authorities had put a political cap on my husband's head. According to them, he was one who "had made a serious political blunder." Because the cap was on my husband's head, it was also on mine. We both had political stains in our personal affairs files. We left the police board partly with a sense of joy and partly with a sense of futility. Walking home, my husband said to me, "We should praise God because He has spared our lives. Now our house arrest is over, and we may be able to find jobs for our living. There are still some problems but God has taught us, 'Hold fast of Him and you will see the deeds of God.'"

We thanked God that He had answered our prayer. The authorities had released us, and we were together.

Chapter 9

Serving in Our Homeland

Before we were released we had no regular living space assigned to us because we were legally outlawed. We dared not even ask the housing board for a room. Now that we were freed, we went to the leader of the housing board and asked him to give us back a room of the house that my parents had built. Several of the rooms had been closed by the authorities when the property had been confiscated by the government, and we thought it only fair and right to ask at least for one room as our home.

But the leader angrily challenged my wife, "Who told you to follow your husband who wears the cap of 'serious political blunder'? It was your choice. Now we cannot give you such a nice room for your home. This house now belongs to us, the Chinese people. If you had married a high government official, or a soldier, we could give you a beautiful apartment. Do you know the Chinese proverb: 'Follow a cock if you married a cock, and follow a dog if you married a dog'? You cannot live in this district because it is now reserved for high government officials. Your husband and you are both politically suspicious and unstable elements. We cannot allow you to live in this district. We shall give you a room in a district of the working class; there you will learn the good qualities of working people."

We were hurt by their insults and their arrogance, but as Christians we are asked to follow Jesus in this world, no matter how poor or difficult the circumstances. We had no choice. We moved to the room assigned to us and lived there in the slum quarters for seven and a half years. The room was small, without toilet or bath. We shared a common kitchen with three other families. It was crowded but we got along quite well.

Finding Employment

To earn a living, I now had to find some kind of job. Fortunately the authorities recognized my medical training and gave me a job as a doctor in a hospital. But because of my prison record they did not give me the salary I had been earning before I was arrested. They demoted me to the level of a new doctor just out of school. It was not enough to meet our needs. This was the kind of economic pressure they applied to someone whom they disliked.

At that time in China no one could do any work without the permission of the labor board. All work was under the control of the government. If you did unassigned work, it was a crime. So Min Tsu went to the labor board asking for a job.

The director investigated her credentials, then said to her, "We need musical specialists, teachers, and other workers in the arts. But you have spent time in prison. Your husband has committed serious political blunders. Also you resigned from your previous work. For these reasons we cannot assign you to any musical work. If you need work, you may choose to stitch leather shoes, dig ditches, or do contruction work."

My wife asked, "Do you mean that I should give up my training to do something else that I have never known? Is that a right policy?"

He gave her a cynical smile and said, "Political status comes first. We never use anyone with bad political status even though you have good training. Get out of here! We have work to do."

Our Child

In deep distress Min Tsu came back and told me his harsh words. On the one hand I consoled her, but on the other I was really worried about our future. A new baby, whom we had asked God to give us, would soon be coming into our home. How could I support all the needs with the small salary that had been allowed me? Was there a future for our baby to grow up under such political domination?

Someone suggested that we have an abortion. But as Christians, how could we agree to do that? Life is from God, and we have no right to destroy it. Furthermore, we wanted to have the baby. My brothers and I were all in early middle life, and there were no children in our whole family.

With tears—and some worrying—we asked God to take care of all these concerns. One night I heard a spiritual voice speak to me, clearly and simply. It was the night of September 21, 1972, nearly four months before our child was to be born. The voice said, "Believe and trust." The next morning I told Min Tsu that God had answered our prayer. "Believe and trust" encouraged us. We lived with that promise until the baby was born.

On January 26, 1973, a new little life came from God, and everything went well. God took care of us and my daughter had no special emergencies because she was in good health. My wife was really blessed; there was no fever and no infection so she stayed in the hospital only a few days. We had borrowed money to pay the bill, because Min Tsu had no health insurance since she had no job. We named the little girl "Believing and Trusting." Being so recently frustrated in her own musical career, my wife noticed our little girl's long and strong fingers. She said to me,

"Our little girl is blessed by God with a wonderful pair of hands. They will be well-suited for piano playing when she grows up."

As time went by her skill was evident. We knew again that God keeps His promise to those who are "believing and trusting." His mercy is everlasting and His truth endures to all generations. Glory to His name.

Living Under Suspicion

Because of my political cap, I was spied on all of the time, even at home. The neighbor told us that she was given a police device and ordered to record our conversations and to keep track of when we left the house and when we returned. She also reported everyone who came to our home—even our parents and brothers.

In the hospital where I worked, the political leaders never talked with me. They pretended not to see me and turned their eyes when we faced each other. They looked upon me as a criminal because I had a heavy political "cap." In their estimation they were as white and pure as snow because they came from the working class.

We knew that two of them, the highest political secretary and his assistant, were living immorally with the young lady doctors and the nurses. The assistant was caught one midnight sleeping with a lady doctor in a room of the hospital. When he heard the knocking on the door, he climbed out the window and tried to hide on the roof. When he was caught by hospital guards who shined their flashlights on him, he only lifted his hands and said, "It is I. I am wrong. Punish me, please."

According to the law of that time, such illicit sex behavior was called simply "the problem of life." He was not punished. They said his nature was good because he came from a poor peasant family. His problem was that he had been corrupted by coming in contact with the bourgeois class! After several months he was transferred to another hospital—still considered a very good political leader.

Personal morality was not valued highly. Public pronouncements said that stealing, fighting, sexual crimes, drinking, and murder would not break the foundation of the socialistic system. Therefore such crimes became common all over China. But if anyone spoke out against any government policy, he was punished. He was charged with undermining the foundations of the socialist system.

Lord, How Can I Serve You?

I never voiced my opinions to anyone in the hospital because I knew it was as dangerous as playing with fire. I worked hard every day treating my patients.

But sometimes I asked God: "Lord, how can I serve You instead of only helping men? Do these unbelievers realize that I am doing good for them because I love You? Why should I spend my time in secular work after I have walked through the valley of death for my faith? Shall I give myself only to earthly matters that weigh so lightly on Your scales? When shall I be released to share Your messages and to testify to the glory of Your name?"

God taught me patience by reminding me of Paul's counsel to Christian slaves in the Roman Empire. He taught them that limitations of this kind were not life's greatest problems. His counsel was: "Brethren, let each man remain with God in that condition in which he was called" (1 Cor. 7:24). I knew that the Bible taught us, "Whatever you do, do all to the glory of God" (1 Cor. 10:31). I understood that if I did my daily work for Him, and never for my own profit—or even only to please others—I would be pleasing to Him.

I spent my after-work time in research and writing some medical articles, but because of my political cap, they were not published. The results of the research were good, but the reports were not used. Some people said, "Doctor, why are you suffering such bad luck? You should ask God to help you, otherwise you cannot keep pace with others. Your schoolmates are much further advanced than you."

It seemed true. And I was hurt when I heard others worrying about my misfortune. But it was not bad luck. I was controlled. My situation was controlled because of my previous political problems. I was deliberately shunned and my work disregarded. I was forbidden many ordinary professional advantages for further learning and development. All because of my arrest and imprisonment!

But as I meditated, an inner voice spoke to me, "When the devil oppresses and makes you unfortunate, it shows that you are close to God's side. Whoever faithfully obeys and follows God often does not get worldly prosperity. Jesus was not successful according to the world's standards. And what apostle was successful, as the world counts success?"

These reflections helped me. I praised God that I was so much better off than when I had been in prison. I also told Him that my mind and my will were committed to Him even if all men were against me.

I had seen enough of cruelty, deceit, selfishness, and desire for power and profits that I had no desire for them.

At the same time God showed me how desirable were His love, His righteousness, and His peace and gladness. I was happy that God gave me insight to choose His way in preference to any other path. He taught me, "If a man cleanses himself from these things, he will be a vessel for honor, sanctified, useful to the Master, prepared for every good work" (2 Tim. 2:21). I asked God to use me all the rest of my life.

Better Times for China

Mao died September 9, 1976. Four weeks later, on October 7, the guilty Gang of Four were arrested and put in prison. The dark clouds that covered all of China were beginning to disperse. Life was beginning to return to normal. God was stretching out His righteous hand to correct some of the evils committed by China's leaders. Followers and co-workers of the Gang of Four were being removed from their leading posts. Many of those helpers immediately changed their loyalties and began criticizing their former leaders. These men and women were professional politicians, always grasping for power. They pretended to be civilized and lawful, but their driving ambition was to trample others at will. They still wished to sit in chairs of leadership, even in the name of another kind of politics, if only they could force innocent people to obey them. Such people never change their real minds. We Chinese have a proverb, "It is much easier to move a mountain or a river than to change one's mind."

In October 1978 the police board was reconsidering my case to see if I had received fair treatment. A leader from my hospital came to the board speaking evil against me. She told the police that I was an unstable man in proletarian politics. Because I had relatives abroad, the hospital did not allow me to do any research work for fear the results of the studies would be stolen. In spite of this testimony, the board agreed that my case had been handled unfairly. When the police board agreed to compensate me for their earlier unfair treatment, this leader immediately changed her position. She came to me and said, "I have gone to the police board many times to urge them to compensate you. You suffered in prison, and after your release from prison you were treated unfairly both financially and mentally."

She then told me that I should be thankful to the Chinese Communist Party and to the Hospital Political Organization. She was clearly suggesting that I should thank her because she had been such a good leader.

On December 18, 1978, I was given full vindication by the police board. I was told by the police, "We have re-examined your whole case and have found no reason to have detained you. There is no evidence to show that you committed serious political blunders. The political leader of your hospital came here testifying against you, but her charges are ridiculous. We have decided to give you full clearance. The economy of the whole country has been damaged by the Gang of Four, but we will ask your leader to compensate you with a small sum for the loss of your money and for your lowered salary."

He then handed me the certificate of my vindication.

I thanked God for His mercy. He had given me the promise "Hold fast of Him and you will see the deeds of God." How that promise was being fulfilled! I knew that this vindication was in no way from man. God was at work. He had also fulfilled the promise that He had given to my wife: "Thou preparest a table before me in the presence of mine enemies: thou anointest my head with oil; my cup runneth over."

The clouds were being blown away and the warm sunshine was coming through. We Chinese Christians were expecting that God's love would shine upon our beautiful land, that Christ's true Church would be established firmly and would grow.

God has kept His word. Even in our land, under very difficult circumstances, Christ has built His Church—not of wood and stone, but of faith and sacrifice. There are many good Christians in China. Praise the Lord. Only Jesus knows them all—the living and those who have gone to death for Him.

I remember that years ago in my country it was easier to be known as a Christian. But when it costs less, it meant less. So, if there is a difference today, if there is some special strength among Chinese Christians, it is because of tribulation. Not tribulation in itself, but because of what God does in the midst of persecution when all you can do is to trust and obey. We know from personal experiences the meaning of Jesus' words: "If anyone wishes to come after Me, let him deny himself, and take up His cross, and follow Me" (Mark 8:34). We have known something of the Cross. We know some of the pain. We know also that there is no way to follow Him without it. But every cup from above is good—even the bitter. Thank God for the Cross and for what He has taught us through it.

Chapter 10

Seeking a New Life

On his birthday, March 22, 1978, my wife's adopted father, a medical doctor, was fasting and praying about our future. God spoke clearly to him through Isa. 52:11-12. "Depart, depart, go out from there, touch nothing unclean; go out of the midst of her, purify yourselves, you who carry the vessels of the Lord. But you will not go out in haste, nor will you go as fugitives; for the Lord will go before you, and the God of Israel will be your rear guard." Through this scripture God showed him—and he told us—that he felt God was planning a new life and responsibility for us. He suggested that we apply for passports from our country and for visas to the United States. But neither one was easy.

I prayed about the decision, but I was worried because I was responsible for the support of our family. If I applied for the passports, I would have to resign my job in the hospital because some leaders there would try to hinder my applications. If I resigned and then could not get the passports and visas, what would the future hold for me and for my family? In our country employment was strictly controlled. If you resigned your job it meant that you would lose your position permanently. There would be no chance for you to follow your profession again.

I dared not take that first step. But my wife's adopted father encouraged and prodded me with this admonition from the Bible: "Let not that man expect that he will receive anything from the Lord, being a double-minded man, unstable in all his ways" (Jas. 1:7-8).

I Step Out on Faith

Finally, believing this to be God's will, I resolutely resigned my job. But first I asked God to open the way ahead for His glory. My wife and I went to the police board and made application for passports. If we had looked at the surroundings or thought more about our future, we would have worried more than we did. But God taught us another special lesson: When Jesus calls, you can walk on the water as Peter did.

Usually I say about myself: My flesh is as weak as a worm, but when God's power is on me I can stand firmly. Therefore I wish to expose my weakness to His power and to His favor in order to glorify His name.

At home I prayed at least five times every day that our passports would be granted. One morning I was praying very earnestly, and the Holy Spirit led me to pray deeper and deeper. Then God told me, "If you put yourself under My omnipotent power, nothing is impossible." I thanked God for His promise and for His almighty power. All of that morning I was full of joy and gladness.

But after a month with no progress at all, my old human weakness overcame me and I went out to seek advice from others. I hoped that someone could help me work it out. I thought that I should make some further efforts of my own. I had the time to do it because I was now not employed. During this time of worry God showed me a vision one night. In the vision I saw that all of us had received our passports. But even with this assurance, I pushed ahead using my own ways and methods to replace His great power and His deeds. Then a voice from above rebuked and admonished me, "You have tried to rely on man more than on Me."

I quite understood that this voice was from God, so I knelt down asking for His forgiveness. I regretted that I had been so weak. Fortunately God corrected my way and His rebuke was strong enough to uphold my weak spirit. He worked it out when I stopped trying to do it in my own way, and rested in faith on His promises. My wife also encouraged me not to worry about our future. She reminded me that God had helped me when I was imprisoned. But it was hard. One month had passed, then another and another.

Five months had gone by, when one morning a letter came in the mail telling us to come for our passports and to bring five yen each to pay for the balance due on them.

Tremendous! Passports for my wife, my daughter, and for me—the whole family. They had been granted in spite of the past false political files and in spite of a very deep negative attitude in the police board. We were to be allowed to leave. We praised God for His faithfulness and thanked Him for His promise: "Hold fast of Him, and you will see the deeds of God."

We Need Visas

Getting the passports was one miracle. But the next necessary step was to secure visas from the American Embassy in Peking. It would require another miracle. Before the visa could be granted, it was necessary to have a sponsorship from someone in America.

We had met Mr. Paul Skiles, Dr. Jerald Johnson, and Rev. John Holstead very briefly when they visited China just one month before we got our passports. God had already prepared for us by sending them to China. How miraculous it was! Now we understand why at that time Mr. Skiles' heart was so eager to visit China.

For getting the sponsorship from someone in America, we prayed God to help and to direct us. Then we wrote letters to our relatives in America as well as to Mr. Skiles. Mr. and Mrs. Skiles quickly completed all required documents and mailed them to us with their kind letter of invitation before we got another sponsorship from our relatives. We thanked God for opening the way before us. We knew clearly that God would do His work for us through our very dear brothers and sisters in Him. Then we got permission from a hospital for my advanced study and from a college in Oklahoma for my wife's further training in music.

God's love on earth always needs a human channel; someone who does not just say the words, but who puts His love into action—even costly action. And they do it joyfully, without limits. Thank God that through the love of Christians, God's messages and our testimonies can be shared with others. Thank God that through the love of His people He has opened a new life for us.

Before we went to Peking to apply for the visas, the weather was very cold. In Peking it was 4 degrees below zero, and there was no heat in the trains. My wife's adopted father prayed to God to give him a sign that He would make our journey successful. He prayed for warmer weather. That would be the sign. After his prayer he felt very happy and peaceful in spirit, so he told us to get ready immediately for the trip. Thankfully the weather did become warmer. We stayed in Peking one full week, and the weather was pleasant. The sun shone brightly every day. We had experienced again that "the effective prayer of a righteous man can accomplish much" (Jas. 5:16).

In the waiting room at the American Embassy we were anxious about getting permission for the whole family. There were three people ahead of us, and their requests were for single permissions only. All three had been turned down. I was No. 4. At that moment God impressed my wife to be completely frank, to tell them everything that we wanted. We went in together for the interview and showed the consul all of our completed documents. We told him that we were four persons; our family of three and my wife's mother. We wished to visit our relatives and friends in America.

We had been so sure that it would be impossible to get visas for four persons that we had left our daughter and my mother-in-law at home when we came to Peking. We had told our daughter, who was then only seven years old, to kneel every day with her grandmother and pray for us. She was faithful in her prayers for us, but she went further. She had a request of her own. She asked God not to let her daddy and mommy go without her, not to allow us to be separated. And God answered her prayer.

After the consul asked us several questions, we asked him if we could sign the applications for our daughter and for her grandmother even though they were not present. He replied kindly, "Certainly you may sign for them."

Tremendous! Within minutes we had received permission for all four visas. It was God's power and His gift of love to us. We thanked the consul general, and in our hearts we gave praise to God. He told us to return to pick up the visas at four o'clock that afternoon.

As soon as we left the embassy we telegraphed the good news home. But information got there before our telegram. At 6:30 that morning a beloved Christian sister had fasted and prayed for our success. As she prayed, God revealed to her that He had answered her prayer and that all four of us would be granted visas—and she told our family members. So about eight hours before our telegram arrived, the family had already received the good news.

We returned to the embassy at four o'clock that afternoon, assuming that many persons would be there to pick up visas. But on this day, out of nearly 40 applicants, only we had been accepted. As the Chinese officer handed me the visas he said, "The consul general was crazy today. Your family of four persons were the only ones to receive visas. We do not know what he was thinking. We have never known before of visas being issued to an entire family."

Incredible? It seemed so to the clerks, but the impossibilities were overcome by the power of God. These miracles have made us understand that:

> *Faith, mighty faith, the promise sees,*
>   *And looks to God alone;*
> *Laughs at impossibilities and cries,*
>   *It shall be done!*

After we had returned to our relatives' home in Peking, we gave our testimonies to them and together we thanked God for His miracles. Our own words seemed inadequate to express our gratitude to God, so as we knelt down to pray we sang the words of this psalm set to a Chinese tune:

> *Shout joyfully to the Lord, all the earth.*
> *Serve the Lord with gladness;*
> *Come before Him with joyful singing.*
> *Know that the Lord Himself is God;*
> *It is He who has made us, and not we ourselves;*
> *We are His people and the sheep of His pasture.*
> *Enter His gates with thanksgiving,*
> *And His courts with praise.*
> *Give thanks to Him; bless His name.*
> *For the Lord is good;*
> *His lovingkindness is everlasting,*
> *And His faithfulness to all generations.*
>   (Ps. 100:1-5)

We also wrote the words of this psalm in a letter that we sent to our family members who had prayed for us.

God never denied His promise to us: "Hold fast of Him, and you will see the deeds of God." Praise to His name!

Last Days in China

It was just two days before the Chinese New Year, so we decided to remain in Peking for the holiday with our relatives. It was the first time I had been in Peking. What a wonderful and meaningful New Year it was!

Our week in China's capital was a deeply moving experience. It is a large and severe city with many historical remains and famous buildings. The Great Wall attracted and amazed us.

China is a beautiful land, but damaged by evil. There are hundreds of millions of beautiful people, created by God, but many are being destroyed both in spirit and in body by the devil.

It was with solemn minds and heavy hearts that we prepared to leave our dear land and her people. We would be leaving most of our family, together with many relatives and friends. Would we ever return to our dear land and to our people? We pray that God will someday restore His Church in China and that the church will live permanently under His direction. We pray that God will bless our nation and save our people.

We bought air tickets to San Francisco, with a stopover in Japan where we planned to visit friends. We were permitted to take only $20.00 in American money, and 25 pounds of luggage for each person.

My wife and I had a very clear and strong invitation from Mr. and Mrs. Paul Skiles in Kansas City, but it was given before anyone knew there would be four of us. According to our Chinese custom, it would be very impolite to arrive with more guests than the host invited or expected. So these questions came to my mind: Where would we go? Where should we live? Was it possible for me to find a job while I was taking advanced study in the hospital? I have a wife, a seven-year-old daughter, and an aged mother-in-law; can I make a living for them in America?

Question after question crossed my mind, but I could not answer them. I told Jesus, "You know the whole situation of yesterday, today, and tomorrow. I do not know even the next minute what will happen to us. I know it is not worthwhile to worry about the future, but Lord—please hold us fast."

If we had not been trusting God and counting on His mercy, we would not have dared to start the trip. Though we had some relatives and some friends in America, for the most part we would be strangers in a strange land. Had we worried about the future, we would have been downcast and discouraged. But God had already stretched out His hands to lead us through the valley of the shadow of death. We could trust Him to guide us on our way.

A good Christian sister prayed with us about our future. God revealed His word to her from the Scripture: "I urge you therefore, brethren, by the mercies of God, to present your bodies a living and holy sacrifice, acceptable to God, which is your spiritual service of worship. And do not be conformed to this world, but be transformed by the renewing of your mind, that you may prove what the will of God is, that which is good and acceptable and perfect" (Rom. 12:1-2).

Inspired by the Holy Spirit to comfort us, she said, "Go ahead, and fear not; God will take care of all of you." We felt happy because God had given us this assurance. It was a very important lesson for us to know that we should ask earnestly, and then wait for His clear answer before we walked into the unknown ahead of us.

On March 7, 1980, we were ready for departure. The airplane was waiting to take us over the sea. Our family and friends were in the airport. Nearly everyone was silent and serious, but we felt secure in the will of God. We shook hands and hugged each other. There were tears in our eyes as each one sang in his own spirit, "God be with you 'til we meet again."

We spent one week in Tokyo, where we were warmly welcomed by some Japanese doctors. They showed us the scenic spots and places of historical interest in Tokyo. We were also asked to visit the Medical Research Center and hospitals.

March 14, we took a Pan Am plane for America. As we flew across the Pacific, the attendants served dinner. We prayed before we ate, and my daughter was frightened. She pushed her mother and whispered, "Mom, do not forget to pray secretly; otherwise you will be put in prison again. Do you remember you taught me to do this? Why have you forgotten?"

With joy Min Tsu told her, "Now we are free. We can pray publicly because there is no trouble any more. It is a blessing from God. Do not be afraid, my little spirit. Pray wherever and whenever and whatever you wish."

My own heart was filled with praise to God for His faithfulness and His kindness. I could only join the Psalmist in his glad song:

They cried out to the Lord in their trouble;
He saved them out of their distresses.
He brought them out of darkness and the shadow of death,
And broke their bands apart.
Let them give thanks to the Lord for His lovingkindness,
And for His wonders to the sons of men!

(Ps. 107:13-15)

Chapter 11

America

After a 14-hour flight, our plane arrived safely at the San Francisco airport. The beloved Christian brother who had helped my wife during her flight from the authorities was there to meet us! His wife and two small boys came with him. Words could not express our thankfulness that by God's mercy we were meeting each other in America. We decided to stay in their home because we thought they would understand our situation better than relatives and other friends from whom we had been separated for more than 30 years. Eagerly we shared our testimonies of the ways God had led us. They treated us as warmly as though we were brother and sisters.

"What is your next step?" they asked. "Where are you going to live? If you wish to stay with us, for the sake of Jesus, we are willing to let you live and work with us. We will make every effort to help you get your permanent visas."

We thanked them, and we thanked God for their love and for their warm words. The offer was especially moving because they were not well off financially. We told them, "We do not know the next step, but we will ask God to open the way ahead and show us what are His arrangements. We are learning to live by faith one day at a time. We are learning from Abraham who 'went out, not knowing whither he went.'"

We asked God to bless this kind Christian family according to His promise: "Whoever gives you a cup of water to drink because of your name as followers of Christ, truly I say to you, he shall not lose his reward" (Mark 9:41).

Kansas City

We received a long-distance call from Mr. Paul Skiles and God's plan was made clear again. Mr. and Mrs. Skiles strongly urged us to come to Kansas City and make our home with them. He assured us, "You are all very welcome. Everything has been arranged, so do not hesitate, and do not delay."

In our spirits we said Amen and decided to go forward. Then more questions came to our minds. How could we adjust to brothers and sisters of a different race, with different customs, and a different culture? It would be very new and strange for us. But we rested in the knowledge that any Christian, anywhere in the world, is God's child. We would be members of the same family in Christ.

Early in the morning of March 19, our Chinese brother took us to the airport. We hugged each other and said good-bye. This would begin a new chapter in our lives in America.

We arrived at the Kansas City International Airport at 4:30 in the afternoon and were met by Mr. and Mrs. Skiles and some close friends. As we were introduced to each other, Mrs. Skiles gave flowers to my wife and her mother and a small doll to my daughter. How excited we were when Miss Mary Scott said, "Welcome, friends. How are you?"—speaking in Chinese. Then we learned that she had been a missionary to China.

Soon we arrived at the Skileses' home. Before we entered, Mr. Skiles handed me a house key, on a key ring engraved with the words "Church of the Nazarene." He said, "This is the key to your new home. It's ours together. Your permanent home where you may live. You are welcome among us. Your coming here is a great blessing."

We thanked God and we thanked them for these kind words. Thus we began our new life in America—with so many things to learn! Each day we read the Bible and pray together. Many Christian brothers and sisters came to greet us warmly and to get acquainted with us.

Free to Worship

March 23, 1980, was an unforgettable Sunday for us who had been lost to public worship for more than 20 years. We went to the Overland Park Church of the Nazarene. Rev. and Mrs. Dennis Johnson welcomed us. As we sat in the sanctuary my heart was filled with praise, and my eyes were filled with tears. I was seeing the vision fulfilled that God had given to me in the prison hospital. He had showed me that I would worship with yellow-haired and brown-haired Christians! I remembered, too, that the devil had tried to pull me out of God's love and care. He had told me that I could go abroad and find success in the world only if I denied Jesus.

My heart was blessed as I listened to the beautiful choir and the sound of the pipe organ. Min Tsu whispered to me, "God's promise to me in the vision of a church, just three days after your release from prison, has been brought to pass. Oh, the music is so beautiful!"

After being so long starved for public worship, we knew how the Psalmist felt when he sang:

How lovely are Thy dwelling places, O Lord of hosts!
My soul longed and even yearned for the courts of
the Lord;
My heart and my flesh sing for joy to the living
God ...
For a day in Thy courts is better than a thousand
outside.

*I would rather stand at the threshold of the house of
my God,
Than dwell in the tents of wickedness.
For the Lord God is a sun and shield;
The Lord gives grace and glory;
No good thing does He withhold from those who
walk uprightly.
O Lord of hosts,
How blessed is the man who trusts in Thee!*
(Ps. 84:1-2, 10-12)

Sharing Our Testimony

Mr. and Mrs. Skiles asked us to stay in Kansas City and seek to become established here instead of going to Oklahoma. We agreed to that. In Mr. Skiles' home we began to tell how God had helped us while we were in our terrible ordeal. Christian brothers and sisters listened to our testimonies with deep sympathy and tears. God had begun to release His messages and the story of His deeds through us. Friends urged us to spend time writing the story so as to give greater glory to our Almighty God.

A Little Miracle in America

One night a patch of my hair on the upper left side of my head came out. We Chinese say it is like "getting your hair cut by a ghost." We consider it a shame for a man to have a bald spot among these healthy hairs. I prayed God to give them back for His name. I asked Him with Christ's promise: "The very hairs of your head are all numbered." I knew that my hairs had been lost and I believed that it was known to God. I believed that He could make them grow again. After several months the lost hairs came back gradually and completely. I am thankful. Do you believe that the very hairs of your head are all numbered?

Light for Our Way

The next necessary step for us was to get permission to remain in the United States legally. We did not know how God would open the way for us, and we could be deported if we did not get permission to remain. Also, we could not impose on our friends indefinitely. We were thankful to God for His special temporary arrangements and for using us—but we were living a very unusual life. What was the next step?

On May 18, 1980, God revealed a vision to me showing my future work in America. I saw two church buildings. Around the edges of their roofs were many lightbulbs. Suddenly these bulbs lighted brightly, but I did not understand what it meant. Then I saw Maxine Skiles standing in front of me. I asked her what it meant. She replied, "It means that you can work now."

Then the vision disappeared, but I was confident that we were going to be able to stay longer in America. The next morning I told Mr. and Mrs. Skiles about the vision. There were some problems to overcome, but I felt God had answered my prayer. And through this vision He had showed me that Sister Maxine had been chosen by Him to help us. We would trust Him for everything.

Nine months later on February 7, 1981, we got the permission from the immigration office. Our visas were all changed from visitor classification to Preliminary Work Permission. The vision was fulfilled.

In June 1980 we moved to a house that was provided for us for six months by Mr. and Mrs. Roy Davis. They said when they first saw us in the Overland Park church, God had spoken to them and told them to help us this way. Other Christian friends helped us to move into our new home. We do not know how to express our gratitude to them all, but we have asked God to reward them for their love and care for us.

During these months God was using us to honor His name in America. I have received many letters from those who have heard our story. They testify that through this witness, God is helping them to change their lives and to reevaluate their services for Christ and His Church. We thank God for His great plan in which He helped us in our troubles and has worked through us to help others.

In a vision the night of June 10, 1980, God revealed to me that Mr. Skiles was to be a teacher of my spirit. In the vision he was teaching me to sing a gospel song. The words were:

> *Fame and wealth are unreal,*
> *Prosperity is vain,*
> *We should forsake them all.*

I understood clearly that God was helping me to learn to take precautions against fame or wealth as I was starting to serve Him in America. At the same time He showed me once again that Mr. Skiles was a good teacher and that I could place my full confidence in him when I had any problem.

We are sure that Mr. and Mrs. Skiles were clearly chosen by God to help us, because He gave us two visions concerning them. They love us very much, and we love them. We shall esteem their costly love forever. Our circle of new Christian brothers and sisters has grown quickly. We appreciate deeply every good Christian who has shown love toward us.

In America we have learned many lessons of Christian love. In response we are seeking to learn how to become love channels to those who need Christ's help. May God's love from heaven flow through His children to earth! May His will be done on earth as it is in heaven!

Chapter 12

He Has Taught Us

In this closing chapter I wish to share some personal impressions of what I have learned about God from our experiences.

Growing Through Suffering

There are many kinds of suffering, but every pain can be profitable to those who believe in Christ. Some Christians suffer as a result of former sins. Although this is suffering of low value, God wants to ease the pain and make it profitable to us. We may recall how much greater our sorrow would have been if we had not found Christ when we did. Thus, even this suffering can be a part of God's discipline that He uses to help us share His holiness.

Some will not leave their evil ways until sin brings such suffering that they realize their error. Thus they are moved to forsake their sinful ways. God uses His rod to discipline men and to turn them into His ways of righteousness.

If we meet this kind of trouble, let us not be stubborn or stiff-necked. Let us examine ourselves under His light and humbly confess our sins. He is faithful and just to forgive our sins and to cleanse us from all unrighteousness.

Suffering for strengthening. Sometimes suffering comes so that God can purify and build us up before He uses us. Before Joseph became the ruler of Egypt, he suffered bitterly.

It is always difficult to understand this kind of suffering at the time that it occurs. We cannot foresee the future and thus cannot know what God is getting us ready to do for Him. We are inclined to sigh because of our misfortune. But we can be sure of this, if God allows trouble to come, He plans for us to be victorious in the struggle. He gives us His promise: "After you have suffered for a little, the God of all grace, who called you to His eternal glory in Christ, will Himself perfect, confirm, strengthen and establish you" (1 Pet. 5:10).

Suffering for testing. Sometimes God tests us to know whether He can trust us to be faithful to Him under greater stresses than we have thus far known. Many people today, like the 5,000 who were fed by Jesus, follow Him for His loaves and fish. They follow Him for His earthly blessings and for His help with their earthly needs. God is concerned about these needs. But in our discipleship Jesus wants to lead us beyond material blessings. Until we get beyond living for things of this world, we are not yet true disciples of Christ. Our goal as Christians is to know Christ in His fullness; to follow Him, to think His thoughts, to do His work, to suffer—if need be—to see His work accomplished. Can I say with Paul, "I count all things to be loss in view of the surpassing value of knowing Christ Jesus my Lord . . . that I may know Him, and the power of His resurrection and the fellowship of His sufferings, [even to] being conformed to His death" (Phil. 3:8, 10)? Only when we are thus ready to suffer with Him can Christ say to us as He said to Peter, "Upon this rock I will build my church; and the gates of Hades shall not overpower it" (Matt. 16:18).

I will be frank to tell you that I did not always know Jesus as well as now. Suffering has opened my spiritual eyes and sharpened my spiritual ears to understand Him more clearly. That new understanding is a blessed experience. To confirm it and enlarge it, I often repeat the prayer of Psalm 139:23-24: "Search me, O God, and know my heart; try me and know my anxious thoughts; and see if there be any hurtful way in me, and lead me in the everlasting way."

The Church Cleansed

In the past, China had many Christians in name but not so many in fact. When suffering came and there were no material benefits from the church, many turned quickly to worldly power. The number of church members dropped. But by suffering, the real Chinese Church has been purified. It now stands firmly on the Rock, Christ Jesus. The Church has been established more firmly than ever before because of her suffering. There are many faithful and respected Chinese Christians; we appreciate them and love them. Trials could not destroy the Church because there was an inner strength to support and to hold up every faithful Christian. This strength is not their own. It comes from God.

Do You Need Strength?

If you are a Christian but you are still not quite sure that you stand firmly upon the Rock, would you ask God to show you the way? If you feel that you could not remain true through suffering, would you ask God to draw you closer to himself? If the trial is too heavy for us to bear, God is merciful and He will open a way for us to go. He will not lead us into trials that are outside of His plans and that cannot add to our strength. After the trial has gone, our spiritual life will be stronger. We shall find ourselves willing to cast aside some things that we once thought we could not give up. We shall be so purified that our communion with God is closer than ever before.

Therefore, let us be at ease when we are suffering. Let us believe and trust Christ fully. If we do not lose our faith, we shall not lose our strength. This faith is the difference between believers and unbelievers. We believers have strength in our spirits, therefore we have peace. God promises us, "As thy days, so shall thy strength be" (Deut. 33:25, KJV).

Suffering Persecution

Persecution for the sake of righteousness seems uncommon in Christian lands today. However, across the centuries many have suffered for doing good. They have been persecuted for protecting the innocent and resented for challenging injustice. Jeremiah called the Jews to repent for disobeying the commands of God. But his king not only refused to obey; he arrested Jeremiah and put him in prison. John the Baptist reproved Herod for the sin of marrying the wife of his brother. For this, John was put in prison and then beheaded.

These men of God suffered for the sake of righteousness. They were persecuted because they spoke out against wrong. They did not fear the authority of evil rulers, and they would rather support the truth than protect their own lives. But the prophets knew their job. God had set them to be guardians of righteousness. Others might keep silence but they could not. Jesus praised these faithful prophets and supported their action when He said, "Blessed are those who have been persecuted for the sake of righteousness, for theirs is the kingdom of heaven" (Matt. 5:10).

Persecution for the work of Christ and in the name of our Lord is the most valuable form of suffering. Every Christian should have some share in these experiences. If our Christian faith does not bring us into conflict with evil or worldliness perhaps our life-style is not enough like Jesus. He tells us that at the end of the world, "They will deliver you to tribulation, and will kill you, and you will be hated by all nations on account of My name" (Matt. 24:9). There are Christians in many lands today who know that not all such persecution lies in the future. We are not to seek for suffering, but we are expected to be aggressively Christian—and we are not to shun suffering when following Christ brings us into conflict with a world that opposes Him.

There is a gladness in our spirits when we suffer for the name of Jesus. Such joy comes in no other way. God may console us when we suffer from other causes, but only he who suffers for Christ finds both consolation and happiness. Peter could testify, "If you are reviled for the name of Christ, you are blessed, because the Spirit of glory and of God rests upon you" (1 Pet. 4:14). Jesus says, "Blessed are you when men cast insults at you, and persecute you, and say all kinds of evil against you falsely, on account of me. Rejoice, and be glad, for your reward in heaven is great, for so they persecuted the prophets who were before you" (Matt. 5:11-12).

Finding Peace

Renouncing self in the face of trouble and drawing back into Christ brings His peace. The real reason that we suffer when we are in trouble is that we still have desires and love for ourselves. Those who die with Jesus may have trouble but they have no pain. Pain is from inside, but trouble is from outside. Too often we try to get rid of trouble by changing the environment. But in doing this we only replace our present pain with another one. Trouble can be released sometimes by human efforts, but pain of the heart is cured only by God. In every time of trouble Christ promises, "These things I have spoken to you, that in Me you may have peace. In the world you have tribulation, but take courage; I have overcome the world" (John 16:33).

Living in Christ

Many Christians have not let their faith really transform their lives. They have accepted Jesus as Savior but have not made Him Lord and Senior Partner. They may read the Bible and pray. They may even go to church every Sunday and give their tithes to support the church. But if you live close to them, you find that their lives have not been radically changed. They are not yet living in Christ.

Before we find this closer fellowship with God, we are self-centered. Even our Christian life revolves around ourselves. We believe in Jesus because we wish to gain eternal life. We study or work hard because we want a comfortable life. Sometimes we pray very earnestly because we hope to get what we need for ourselves. In making our decisions and solving our problems we rely on ourselves. We seldom ask God what is His will for us. We have come to know Christ, but we are not yet living in Him.

In this relationship to Christ we are subject to failure and sin. Because we do not rely on His guidance we sometimes do wrong without knowing it. Because we do not rely on God's power we sometimes know what is wrong but we are not able to overcome it.

How can one be a Christian for many years and his life still not be basically changed? The answer is that we need to go deeper with Christ. It is good to begin the Christian life; but it is bad to stop short of full commitment to God and to fail to live in full fellowship with Him.

How do we move ahead from knowing Christ as Savior to the deeper level of making Him Lord of our lives? The change occurs most often when we hear Bible teaching on entire sanctification. Having heard that message, we respond to Jesus' command to tarry until our lives are filled with His Holy Spirit. If we have not heard this Bible teaching, God can lead us into this deeper Christian life as we respond to His voice. That is how God led me into this life-changing experience.

One day we find ourselves in a situation where we know that we must have more help from Jesus than we have ever had before. We cannot follow His way in our own strength. In this hour we earnestly ask for His deliverance.

At that time God opens our inner eyes, and His light comes into our hearts in a new way. We can now understand Him more clearly, and we rely more fully on His power. Our spiritual eyes are opened and we know clearly the way He wants us to go. We are amazed at how little we saw and how dark it was before our inner eyes were opened. We repent and ask God's forgiveness for our weakness and failure. We confess our need for a closer walk with Him. We ask Him to show us what He wants us to do. If we are fully open to His will He shows us our need, and He fills us with His Holy Spirit.

This deeper encounter with God is followed by real life changes. Our thinking, our speaking, and our doing will be quite different from what they were before. We understand more fully that there is no grace, or blessing, or deliverance, or hope without Jesus. Living in Him we find His peace, His happiness, His fellowship, and His guidance. It may seem something of a mystery until we experience it, but it is real. Of his own experience Paul writes, "I have been crucified with Christ; and it is no longer I who live, but Christ lives in me; and the life which I now live in the flesh I live by faith in the Son of God, who loved me, and delivered Himself up for me" (Gal. 2:20).

Living in Christ means listening to what God says and obeying what He asks. I thank God that He led me personally into this experience. If we had not found this deeper life with Him, we would not be alive today.

Praying in the Spirit

Sometimes I am asked, "How can we get the words directly from God? How does God reveal His will through visions?"

First I wish to say that this form of revelation is a gift from God; and He gives His gifts to different persons in different forms. He may also reveal His will to us in different ways.

However, we know that God is a revealing God. He wants to have fellowship with us and to make His will known to us. He has revealed himself in many ways. Before we had a written Bible, God said, "To any prophet among you I make myself known by visions, I talk to him in dreams. Not so with my servant Moses, so faithful in all my household; I speak to him directly, openly, with no dark sayings, and he sees the very form of the Eternal" (Num. 12:6-8, Moffatt).

But in our day we have the Scriptures and the teachings of Jesus. Even so, the Bible usually gives us only general or universal guidelines. Only God himself can show us His special will for our individual lives. For this purpose He sent His Holy Spirit into the world, and He sends Him into our lives. Jesus promised, "When He, the Spirit of truth, comes, He will guide you into all the truth" (John 16:13). He wants us to know. He invites us to ask. He assures us that His Holy Spirit will lead us.

It is not ours to dictate how God's Spirit shall reveal His will to us. It is ours to ask for His guidance. It is His sovereign decision to choose how He brings certainty to our spirits. You may receive your guidance in ways different from mine.

But there are conditions that we must all meet if we are to receive God's gift of guidance. If we wish to pray in the Spirit, we must live in the Spirit. We must be sure that our spirits have been cleansed by His blood. Jesus promised His followers, "If you abide in Me, and My words abide in you, ask whatever you wish, and it shall be done for you" (John 15:7). It is a staggering promise, and we do not know all that it means, but of this we are sure: if we are to receive guidance from Him, we must abide in Him.

The second step is to pray in the Spirit. God is a Spirit; we communicate with Him spirit to Spirit. My personal experiences of praying in the Spirit have made me very happy and peaceful. God was so near and so real to me that I was not willing to stop my praying.

I have learned that it takes time to come to God in spirit. It is impossible to experience Him in this way by praying only a few minutes. If God is to communicate profoundly to us, we must spend much time in His presence. We Christians are servants of God. We need to pray for God's work, for other Christians, for lost souls, for our country, and for the whole world. All need our love and support through prayer.

Why do I emphasize spending much time in prayer? Because I have learned that we cannot overcome our enemies except by keeping close to Jesus, our Lord. If we are not close to Him, we are in danger every hour. The Bible exhorts us, "You, beloved, building yourselves up on your most holy faith; praying in the Holy Spirit; keep yourselves in the love of God" (Jude 20-21).

The Worth of His Word

God tells us, "Blessed is he who reads and those who hear the words of the prophecy, and heed the things which are written in it; for the time is near" (Rev. 1:3). I testify that the verse has been true in our lives. As we have learned His will from the Bible and have followed His guidance, we have been blessed.

His Word is sweet! Before I was put in prison I read the

Bible every day as a part of my schedule. Sometimes I read it carefully but sometimes I read it in a hurry. I did not realize how fortunate I was to have God's Word until we lost the Bible. In China at that time it was illegal to read a Bible or to sing a hymn. There came to us the feeling of hunger and thirst for His Word, such a feeling I had never known before. We had come upon the day of which the prophet wrote:

> *A famine on the land,*
> *Not a famine for bread or a thirst for water,*
> *But rather for hearing the words of the Lord.*
> (Amos 8:11)

I regretted that I had not memorized many more verses and chapters. I recalled from memory as much of God's Word as I possibly could. But it was never enough. I loved the Word that I had because it was so sweet, but I had lost God's Book.

I know a Christian who traded his watch for a New Testament. In that farming area a watch cost a year's salary. At the same exchange rate a small New Testament would cost $10,000 in America. Chinese Christians value the Bible. We have experienced the bitterness of losing God's Word, so we have known the sweetness of recovering the Bible.

I have never heard of a person crying tears of joy when he recovered a lost book. But I have seen such an outpouring of emotion from a strong man when he got a Bible—even a very small one—after he had been deprived of God's Word for more than 10 years.

His Word gives courage! When everything is peaceful we are usually not so aware of our need of help from God. But we turn to Him in the time of wind and storm. Therefore God does not allow His children to live always in a pleasant environment. It is better to find God in a storm that to lose Him on a sunny day.

In my trouble I began to know God's voice and to understand the importance of obeying His Word. If I had not heard His voice, I could not have tolerated my suffering in jail. That Word became my life and my strength. No other voice in the world could have saved me at that time. His living and powerful Word led me through the valley of the shadow of death.

His Word is powerful! God's Word can support and console a broken heart. Without the help of God's brief words of guidance, I would have gone out of my mind in the jail. Without the help of God's Word, my wife and I would not be alive today.

Without the help of God's revelation to His Chinese children, all the lights in China would have gone out during the darkest and hardest times there. Without His help, the Chinese Church would not have survived. But thanks to our God, because of His powerful Word, His Church in China is growing and prospering. Because He is with His Church, and because she has His Word, "the gates of hell shall not prevail against it" (Matt. 16:18, KJV).

His Word is faithful! Jesus is the same yesterday, today, and forever. He never loses His power. By His word the heavens and the earth were created; everything in them is under His control. At the end of the world even the heavens and the earth will pass away, but not one dot or one dash of His Word will be changed. His Word is faithful and will remain so forever. His truth endures to all generations because He cannot deny himself.

If you have met with some things that you do not understand, believe and trust Him. Do not worry or be doubtful because He will not fail you. This is my testimony.

The Battle with Ease

I know that the battle with the devil is not limited to the kind of trials that we went through in China. I have known some Christians who stood firmly in hard times but they went down in easier days.

The devil does not seem to use martyrdom in his battle against the Church in Western countries. But he uses another very effective attack. Freedom is a good word, but if we think of freedom as a right to do whatever pleases us, we should recognize that this is a form of Satan's appealing and subtle attack.

The church in Smyrna (Rev. 2:8-11) suffered fiery tribulation. It was the violent form of Satan's attack, and they stood firm against it. But the church of Laodicea (Rev. 3:14-22) failed because they had it too easy and her people were too self-satisfied. Laodicea was the only one of the seven churches that received no commendation from Christ.

The church at ease is in great danger because the world easily comes into such a church. The children of God then follow the trends of the world, the church compromises, and her people almost unconsciously become like the world.

The devil thus has two faces; but he has only one purpose. Whether by the violence of persecution or by the seduction of an easy life, Satan proposes to draw us away from God.

A Final Word

I trust that our lessons of blood and tears have been a help to you but I ask you to forget the persons in the book; look only upon the One who led us through the valley of the shadow of death. Ask Him to lead you also just where He wants you to go. Ask Him to reveal himself to you—to reveal His reality, His goodness, and His purposes for your life.

A Chinese sister said, "Naturally, no one wishes to be imprisoned, but if that were necessary to enjoy Christ's sweetness and His presence, I would be willing to remain in jail." Chinese Christians are still fighting strongly against the devil in their spiritual war. They need the support of your prayers and your remembrance. Please pray for them, and ask God to give them strength to overcome the evil one.

Christians in our age at the end of the world should prepare for the darkness. There will be many tribulations and destructive heresies. Let us watch and pray, asking God to help us. Let us trust and obey His Word. Let us love each other fervently from the heart. Let us gird our minds for action, keep sober in spirit, and place our hope completely on the grace to be brought to us at the revelation of Jesus Christ. Let us sacrifice ourselves for Him. Jesus tells us, "Truly, truly, I say to you, unless a grain of wheat falls into the earth and dies, it remains by itself alone; but if it dies, it bears much fruit" (John 12:24).

Recently I have been taught by His voice to my spirit, "Before you are taken up into glory, you must keep on going the way of the Cross, as Jesus did when He was on earth."

I believe that He is coming again very soon. I ask you to be challenged by His word, "I urge you therefore, brethren, by the mercies of God, to present your bodies a living and holy sacrifice, acceptable to God, which is your spiritual service of worship" (Rom. 12:1).

I Testify

The following words of Scripture have often supported me. From my own experiences I bear my glad witness that they are true.

"It is a trustworthy statement, deserving full acceptance, that Christ Jesus came into the world to save sinners, among whom I am foremost of all" (1 Tim. 1:15). It is true.

"If we are faithless, He remains faithful; for He cannot deny Himself" (2 Tim. 2:13). I have found it so.

"But realize this, that in the last days difficult times will come. For men will be lovers of self, lovers of money, boastful, arrogant, revilers, disobedient to parents, ungrateful, unholy, unloving, irreconcilable, malicious gossips, without self-control, brutal, haters of good, treacherous, reckless, conceited, lovers of pleasure rather than lovers of God; holding to a form of godliness, although they have denied its power; and avoid such men as these" (2 Tim. 3:1-5). I have seen much of this, and I know its danger.

"But remember the former days, when, after being enlightened, you endured a great conflict of sufferings, partly, by being made a public spectacle through reproaches and tribulations, and partly by becoming sharers with those who were so treated. For you showed sympathy to the prisoners, and accepted joyfully the seizure of your property, knowing that you have for yourselves a better possession and an abiding one. Therefore, do not throw away your confidence, which has a great reward. For you have need of endurance, so that when you have done the will of God, you may receive what was promised. FOR YET IN A VERY LITTLE WHILE, HE WHO IS COMING WILL COME, AND WILL NOT DELAY. BUT MY RIGHTEOUS ONE SHALL LIVE BY FAITH; AND IF HE SHRINKS BACK MY SOUL HAS NO PLEASURE IN HIM" (Heb. 10:32-38). It is true.

"Without faith it is impossible to please Him, for he who comes to God must believe that He is, and that He is a rewarder of those who seek Him" (Heb. 11:6). I have found it so.

"In the world you have tribulation, but take courage; I have overcome the world" (John 16:33). He has proved it to me.

"They overcame him because of the blood of the Lamb and because of the word of their testimony, and they did not love their life even to death" (Rev. 12:11). He has done this for us.

Let Us Be True

Dear reader:

"Since we have so great a cloud of witnesses surrounding us, let us also lay aside every encumbrance, and the sin which so easily entangles us, and let us run with endurance the race that is set before us, fixing our eyes on Jesus, the author and perfecter of faith, who for the joy set before Him endured the cross, despising the shame, and has sat down at the right hand of the throne of God" (Heb. 12:1-2).

"Worthy is the Lamb that was slain to receive power and riches and wisdom and might and honor and glory and blessing" (Rev. 5:12).

"Great and marvelous are Thy works, O Lord God, the Almighty; righteous and true are Thy ways, Thou King of the nations. Who will not fear, O Lord, and glorify Thy name? For Thou alone art holy; for ALL THE NATIONS WILL COME AND WORSHIP BEFORE THEE, for Thy righteous acts have been revealed" (Rev. 15:3-4).

"When you pass through the waters, I will be with you; and through the rivers, they will not overflow you. When you walk through the fire, you will not be scorched, nor will the flame burn you. For I am the Lord your God, the Holy One of Israel, your Savior" (Isa. 43:2-3). To these blessed truths we say, Amen and Amen.

Our Commitment

O Lord, we will follow You anywhere that You lead us. You are our Master.

"Who shall separate us from the love of Christ? Shall tribulation, or distress, or persecution, or famine, or nakedness, or peril, or sword? . . . [No] in all these things we overwhelmingly conquer through Him who loved us" (Rom. 8:35, 37).

OUR HEART'S DESIRE

I'd rather have Jesus than silver or gold;
I'd rather be His than have riches untold;
I'd rather have Jesus than houses or lands.
I'd rather be led by His nail-pierced hand.

I'd rather have Jesus than men's applause;
I'd rather be faithful to His dear cause:
I'd rather have Jesus than worldwide fame.
I'd rather be true to His holy name.

He's fairer than lilies of rarest bloom;
He's sweeter than honey from out the comb;
He's all that my hungering spirit needs.
I'd rather have Jesus and let Him lead.

Than to be the King of a vast domain
Or be held in sin's dread sway.
I'd rather have Jesus than anything
This world affords today.*

—Rhea F. Miller

*© Copyright 1922, 1950. © Renewed 1939, by Chancel Music, Inc. Assigned to The Rodeheaver Company (A Div. of Word, Inc.) All rights Reserved. International Copyright Secured. Used by permission.